I0446389

Customer Success Mastery

50 Strategies to Retain Customers, Drive Revenue, and Ignite Business Growth

Jeffrey Rogers

Jeffrey Ray Rogers

Copyright © 2023 by Jeffrey Ray Rogers

All rights reserved.

No portion of this book may be reproduced in any form without written permission from the publisher or author, except as permitted by U.S. copyright law

ISBN: 9798864556634

.

Table of Contents

Table of Contents   **3**

Letter From the Author   **8**

Why Customer Success?   **10**

PART I: THE FOUNDATIONS OF CUSTOMER SUCCESS   **14**

Customer Retention Strategies   **15**

The Customer-Centric Approach   **26**

The Data-Driven Customer Retention Strategy   **32**

PART II: CUSTOMER UNDERSTANDING AND SEGMENTATION   **38**

Voice of the Customer Programs   **39**

Customer Journey Mapping   **47**

Customer Feedback and Satisfaction Surveys   **54**

Net Promoter Score   **62**

Customer Health Score   **70**

Customer Segmentation   **76**

Customer Personas   **81**

Customer Acquisition Strategies: Balancing Growth and Retention   **89**

PART III: CUSTOMER SUCCESS STRATEGIES   **94**

The Importance of Onboarding and Implementation Processes 95

High-Touch, Low-Touch, and Tech-Touch Strategies 104

Upselling and Cross-Selling 113

Customer Loyalty Programs 119

Referral Programs 124

Customer Education and Training Programs 131

PART IV: BUILDING CUSTOMER RELATIONSHIPS 136

Quarterly and Annual Business Reviews 137

Thought Leadership and Content Marketing 144

Public Speaking and Event Participation for Customer Success Managers 151

Partnerships and Alliances 158

Customer Advisory Boards 164

Industry Research and Benchmarking 170

PART V: DATA-DRIVEN CUSTOMER SUCCESS 176

Utilizing Customer Data Analytics and Insights for Successful Customer Success Strategies 177

Capturing and Reporting on Customer Success Metrics and KPIs 186

Continuous Improvement and Innovation 192

Churn Analysis 199

Root Cause Analysis   203

Data-Driven Decision-Making in Customer Success   210

PART VI: CUSTOMER SUPPORT AND TECHNOLOGY 219

Types of Customer Support Channels and How to Implement Them for
Exceptional Customer Experience   220

Self-Service Portals   227

Chatbots and AI-Powered Customer Service   233

Customer Success Management Software   237

Customer Relationship Management and Marketing Automation
Integration   245

PART VII: ENGAGEMENT AND TEAM BUILDING 252

Personalization and Customization   253

Agile Development Methodologies   259

DevOps and Continuous Delivery   265

Community Building and Engagement   271

PART VIII: TEAM DEVELOPMENT AND CULTURE 277

Leveraging an Effective Customer Success Team Structure and Roles
                                                              278

Performance Coaching and Development   285

Incentives and Bonuses   296

Gamification and Competition   **305**

Ensuring Communication and Alignment in a Customer Success Team
    311

Leveraging Executive Sponsorship and Buy-In   **317**

Harnessing Company Culture and Values   **326**

Boosting Employee Engagement and Satisfaction   **333**

PART IX: LEADERSHIP AND FUTURE PLANNING 340

Training and Development Opportunities for CSMs   **341**

Leadership and Management Development   **350**

Succession Planning for Customer Success Teams   **358**

Conclusion: Embracing a Customer Success Mindset   **365**

Final Thoughts From the Author   **367**

ABOUT THE AUTHOR   **369**

Special Thanks   **371**

Letter From the Author

Dear Reader,

I am thrilled to introduce you to my book, *Customer Success Mastery*. This book is the culmination of my years of experience and expertise in the field of customer success, and it is designed to be your comprehensive guide to mastering the art and science of ensuring customer satisfaction, loyalty, and growth.

I understand that your time is valuable, and that's why I want to assure you that you do not need to read this book cover to cover. Instead, I encourage you to use it as a valuable resource to explore specific topics and subjects that pique your interest or align with the specific needs and challenges you face in your customer success role. Whether you are a seasoned customer success professional looking to refine your strategies or someone new to the field seeking foundational knowledge, there's something in these pages for everyone.

This comprehensive guide is divided into nine sections, each designed to empower you in the realm of customer success. From foundational principles and practical strategies to leveraging robust relationships, data-driven insights, technology, engagement, team development, and leadership planning, this book is your versatile toolbox for addressing specific challenges and finding inspiration throughout your customer success journey.

Remember, dear reader: this book is not meant to be read from start to finish. Feel free to navigate the chapters and explore topics that resonate with you. It is a reference book, a resource full of ideas and strategies that you can draw from whenever you seek inspiration or need solutions to challenges you encounter in your customer success journey.

I encourage you to approach this book with an open mind, ready to absorb knowledge and consider new ideas. The insights you gain from these pages will empower you to elevate your customer success efforts, amplify customer satisfaction, and drive exceptional growth within your organization.

Thank you for joining me on this enlightening adventure. May this book be your guide, your source of inspiration, and your catalyst for positive change in your customer success department. Together, let us unlock the true potential of customer-centric business and create remarkable experiences for our customers.

I wish you boundless success and meaningful connections.

Jeffrey Ray Rogers, CISSP, CISA, MIS, CEH, CHFI
VP of Customer Success and Global Support

Why Customer Success?

In an age marked by relentless competition and the ever-evolving demands of customers, the concept of "customer success" has become more than just a buzzword; it's an essential strategy that distinguishes thriving businesses from the rest. Customer success isn't merely a department within an organization; it's a fundamental approach that needs to permeate every facet of a company's operations.

Customer Retention: The Bedrock of Success

One of the most compelling reasons to prioritize customer success is its direct impact on customer retention. It's no secret that retaining existing customers is often more cost-effective than acquiring new ones. A loyal customer base not only provides a stable revenue stream but also serves as a foundation for sustainable growth. When customers feel valued and supported throughout their journey, they are more likely to remain loyal to a brand. Customer success plays a pivotal role in nurturing this loyalty by ensuring customers achieve their desired outcomes and continue to derive value from the products or services they've invested in.

Revenue Growth From Existing Customers

While attracting new customers is essential for business expansion, existing customers are an invaluable asset for driving revenue growth. Customer success isn't solely about keeping customers satisfied; it's also about identifying opportunities for upselling and cross-selling. When customers have a positive experience and trust in a company's offerings, they are more receptive to exploring additional products or services that can enhance their experience or address their evolving needs. Customer success teams, armed with a deep understanding of customer preferences and behaviors, are well-positioned to identify and capitalize on these opportunities, contributing significantly to revenue growth.

Responsive Customer Support

Exceptional customer support is a hallmark of any successful business. However, the traditional model of reactive support, where companies primarily respond to customer issues and complaints, is no longer sufficient. Customers now expect proactive and responsive support that addresses their needs even before they recognize them.

Customer success encompasses this evolving paradigm by actively engaging with customers, understanding their pain points, and preemptively resolving issues. By embracing a proactive support model, companies can not only prevent customer churn but also foster a positive brand image that attracts new customers.

An Overall Better Customer Experience

Ultimately, customer success is about delivering superior customer experiences. It involves understanding customers' goals, challenges, and expectations and tailoring interactions to meet those needs. When customers consistently have positive experiences with a company, they are more likely to become advocates, spreading the word to friends, family, and peers. Positive word-of-mouth and referrals are invaluable assets for business growth, and they often originate from customers who have benefited from exceptional customer success efforts.

Your Journey Toward Customer Success Mastery

Customer success is not a luxury; it's a necessity in today's business landscape. It's a strategy that revolves around understanding, nurturing, and empowering customers to achieve their goals and derive maximum value from the products or services offered.

By prioritizing customer success, businesses can bolster customer retention, drive revenue growth, provide responsive support, and, most importantly, create a superior overall customer experience. It's a strategy that propels companies toward excellence in an era where customers' expectations are higher than ever before.

Your journey toward customer success is an investment in your company's sustainability and prosperity. It's a commitment to helping your customers succeed and, in turn, securing your own success in an ever-evolving business landscape. The chapters that follow will explore how you can effectively implement and leverage customer success to achieve these goals.

This book is your comprehensive guide to creating and nurturing a successful customer success department. It will delve into the intricacies of customer retention, data-driven strategies, responsive support, and all the techniques that foster better customer experiences.

As you embark on your journey through the following chapters, you will discover a wealth of strategies, best practices, and real-world examples that can elevate your customer success efforts to new heights. Whether you're new to the world of customer success or a seasoned professional, there's something here for everyone.

Get ready to transform your approach to customer relationships, drive revenue growth, and position our company as a leader in customer-centricity. The path to customer success starts here, and the possibilities are limitless.

Part I: The Foundations of Customer Success

"The purpose of a business is to create and keep a customer." — Peter Drucker, Management Consultant

Chapter One
Customer Retention Strategies

As a customer success department, one of your primary goals is to ensure that your company's customers remain loyal and continue to generate revenue over time. To achieve this, you need to have a well-defined customer retention strategy in place.

In this chapter, we will explore some of the most effective customer retention strategies and examine their pros and cons.

Types of Customer Retention Strategy

Customer retention is crucial for enterprise businesses to succeed in the long run. While there are several effective customer retention strategies available, such as customer-centric, data-driven, and loyalty programs, each approach has pros and cons. By carefully considering the strengths and weaknesses of each approach, you can develop a customer retention strategy that is tailored to your business's unique needs and goals.

Let's dive into some of these strategies below.

Customer-Centric Strategy

The customer-centric retention strategy places the customer at the center of all business decisions and actions. When a business understands customer needs and preferences, they can tailor their products and services to meet those needs and create a more personalized experience. This can lead to increased customer satisfaction, loyalty, and retention.

However, implementing a customer-centric strategy requires a significant investment in time, resources, and technology. Additionally, it may not be suitable for all types of businesses or industries, and some customers may still choose to leave despite efforts to retain them. Ultimately, a customer-centric retention strategy must strike a balance between meeting customer needs and achieving business goals.

Pros:

- *Customer satisfaction and loyalty:* When your customers are satisfied with their experiences and loyal to your brand, you'll see less churn and higher customer retention.
- *Positive brand reputation:* By putting the customer first, a company can build a positive brand reputation. This can lead to you gaining new customers through word-of-mouth referrals.
- *Increased revenue:* Happy customers are more likely to spend more money and purchase additional products or services.
- *Competitive advantage:* A customer-centric approach can differentiate a company from its competitors, as it shows a commitment to meeting customer needs and desires.

Cons:

- *High costs:* A customer-centric strategy can be expensive, as it often involves investing in new technology, training staff, and offering personalized services.

- *Time-consuming:* Implementing this strategy can require significant time and effort as it involves collecting and analyzing customer data, implementing new processes, and training staff.
- *High customer demands:* A company may find itself dealing with challenging customer demands and expectations, which can be difficult to fulfill.
- *Risk of losing focus:* Focusing too much on customer needs and neglecting other important aspects of the business, such as financial goals or product innovation, can be harmful to the company.

A customer-centric retention strategy is of paramount importance for enterprise companies due to its potential to drive sustainable growth and long-term success. By prioritizing customer satisfaction and loyalty, businesses can create a strong and reliable customer base. This leads to repeat purchases and increased customer lifetime value (CLV), which is the total amount of revenue a customer generates over their lifetime with your business.

A customer-centric approach fosters trust, enhances brand reputation, and encourages positive word-of-mouth referrals, all of which can significantly impact the company's bottom line. Moreover, understanding and addressing the specific needs of individual customers can lead to tailored solutions and personalized experiences, further strengthening the bond between the company and its customers.

In a highly competitive market where customer acquisition costs are often high, focusing on retaining existing customers proves to be more cost-effective and efficient in the long run. By consistently delivering value and exceptional service, enterprise companies can build lasting relationships and secure a competitive advantage in the market, positioning themselves for sustainable growth and continued success.

Data-Driven Customer Retention Strategy

A data-driven customer retention strategy focuses on analyzing customer data to identify trends, behaviors, and patterns that can help improve customer satisfaction and reduce churn.

One of the key components of this approach is the use of health scores, which provide a way to quantify the overall health of a customer's relationship with a company.

Pros:

- *Predictive churn prevention:* Provides a systematic way to identify customers who are at risk of churning and take proactive steps to prevent it.
- *Personalized customer experiences:* Enables businesses to personalize customer experiences and tailor retention efforts to individual customer needs.
- *Enhanced product development:* Can provide insights into product development and help companies improve customer satisfaction.

Cons:

- *Incomplete customer insights:* A data-driven customer retention strategy may not capture all aspects of customer sentiment and satisfaction, leading to blind spots in retention efforts.
- *Loss of personalization:* A reliance on data and algorithms may lead to a lack of human touch and personalized interaction with customers.
- *Data limitations and bias:* Data can be limited or biased, leading to incorrect assessments and actions.

A data-driven customer retention strategy, including the use of health scores, can be a powerful tool for businesses to improve customer satisfaction and reduce churn. However, it's important to balance data-driven and human insights while considering data limitations and potential biases.

Elements of a Customer Retention Strategy

Whether you opt for a customer-centric retention strategy or a data-driven approach, the key to ensuring lasting success lies in the convergence of several essential elements.

To truly excel in customer retention, it's imperative to weave together the fabric of personalized customer experiences, proactive customer support, loyalty programs, and multifaceted customer engagement campaigns. These components seamlessly bridge the gap between customer-centric and data-driven strategies.

Personalized experiences resonate deeply with customers as they showcase your commitment to their unique needs. Proactive support demonstrates your dedication to their satisfaction, heading off issues before they arise. Loyalty programs foster a sense of belonging and value, while ongoing engagement campaigns keep your brand at the forefront of customers' minds.

When these elements harmonize, whether driven by customer-centric empathy or data-driven precision, you create a customer success strategy that not only retains but genuinely delights customers, fostering long-term growth and profitability for your organization.

Personalized Customer Experience

One of the most potent elements of a customer retention strategy is the provision of a highly personalized experience that caters to the specific and unique needs of each customer. This approach revolves around the art of harnessing customer data and feedback and using them as the building blocks of tailored products, services, and interactions. The beauty of personalization lies in its transformative ability to enhance customer satisfaction and loyalty. When customers feel a brand truly understands their preferences and anticipates their desires, a strong emotional connection is forged.

Personalization can be a game-changer for a company's bottom line. When customers are offered precisely what they are looking for, they are more likely to make repeat purchases and become long-term patrons. This not only increases CLV but also bolsters revenue streams. However, it's important to acknowledge that personalization can be an intricate and resource-intensive endeavor, particularly for businesses with extensive customer bases.

Nonetheless, the investment in personalization pays substantial dividends in the form of increased customer satisfaction, loyalty, and advocacy. Beyond its economic benefits, it fosters a sense of appreciation among customers, making them feel valued and understood. This, in turn, can lead to word-of-mouth referrals and an invaluable reputation for delivering exceptional customer experiences.

Proactive Customer Support

Proactive customer support is a vital component of customer success, as it goes beyond simply addressing issues; it's about preventing them in the first place. This approach involves anticipating and understanding customer needs and then taking proactive steps to meet those needs before they escalate into problems. This strategy is instrumental in dispelling the sometimes confusing distinction between customer support and customer success.

By proactively addressing technical and training needs, this approach to support ensures that customers have a seamless experience with your product or service. This, in turn, frees up your customer success managers to focus on higher-level engagement and consultative services.

The real magic of proactive customer support lies in its potential to prevent customer churn. When you help customers navigate your product or service effectively, steering them clear of major obstacles, you not only enhance their experience but also significantly increase your likelihood of gaining their long-term loyalty.

However, it's important to acknowledge that scaling this proactive approach for larger customer bases can be challenging and may require a substantial investment of time and resources. The investment is often well worth it, as it leads to increased customer retention, higher satisfaction, and a reputation for exceptional customer care — all cornerstones of a thriving customer retention strategy.

Customer Engagement Campaigns

Customer engagement campaigns are invaluable tools in your customer success arsenal. These campaigns are meticulously designed to foster a dynamic relationship with customers, one that transcends mere transactions. By enticing customers to take various actions, such as exploring new use cases, participating in webinars, or finding out about fresh features and products, engagement campaigns serve as catalysts for meaningful interactions.

The main advantage of this approach lies in its capacity to fortify the customer–provider bond. Engaged customers are not just consumers; they are active participants in the product or service experience. Encouraging them to explore different facets of your offering can lead to a more profound understanding of its utility, prompting them to discover new applications they might not have considered otherwise.

Moreover, engagement campaigns have the power to spark conversations. They serve as a bridge for discussions on what the next steps should be in the customer's journey with your product. This collaborative approach aligns your offering more closely with their evolving needs, fostering a sense of partnership.

Perhaps most significantly, engagement campaigns empower customers to become advocates for your company or product. When individuals are engaged and find value in your offering, they naturally become more inclined to share their positive experiences with their network. This word-of-mouth promotion can be an invaluable asset for boosting brand reputation and attracting new customers.

However, it's essential to acknowledge the challenge of quantifying the return on investment (ROI) of engagement campaigns. Unlike some more transactional strategies, the impact of engagement on customer retention is often nuanced and gradual. While it may not yield immediate, easily measurable results, the long-term benefits of strengthened customer relationships, increased product usage, and the advocacy of engaged customers can significantly contribute to enhanced retention rates.

In essence, engagement campaigns are the cornerstone of cultivating customer loyalty. They transform customers into enthusiastic partners, facilitating deeper product adoption and advocacy. Though their impact may not always be immediately quantifiable, their contribution to long-term customer retention is undeniable.

Continuous Improvement

Continuous improvement is the final element of a successful retention strategy. By diligently analyzing your customers' feedback and translating it into tangible product and service enhancements, you're not just addressing their immediate needs and pain points; you're signaling a commitment to their long-term satisfaction. This proactive approach has a ripple effect that extends far beyond resolving current issues.

Firstly, it fosters a sense of partnership between your company and its customers. When customers see that their feedback is not only valued but also acted upon, they begin to perceive themselves as more than just consumers; they become integral partners in your journey toward excellence. This shift in perception breeds loyalty, as customers are more likely to stick with a company that genuinely listens and adapts to their evolving needs.

Moreover, continuous improvement allows you to stay ahead of the curve. Regular interactions with customers unveil new use cases for your products or services, reveal shifting industry dynamics, and gauge evolving customer sentiment. Armed with this knowledge, you can proactively adjust your offerings to remain aligned with the market and customer expectations. This adaptability translates into better customer experiences, as customers are less likely to encounter issues or limitations with your products and more likely to find value that aligns precisely with their evolving requirements.

However, it's crucial to strike a balance between continuous improvement and customization. While striving for uniformity can lead to a disconnect with certain customer segments, it's equally important not to lose sight of the overarching goal: to create products and services that provide value to the majority while maintaining the flexibility to tailor solutions to meet the unique demands of specific demographics or niches. This balanced approach ensures that your continuous improvement efforts not only retain customers but also provide a consistently outstanding customer experience, reinforcing your brand's reputation and competitive advantage in the long run.

Final Thoughts

The customer success department plays a crucial role in the long-term success of a company by fostering customer loyalty and revenue generation. By focusing on ensuring customer satisfaction and building strong relationships, the department can effectively retain existing customers and create a stable revenue stream over time.

A well-defined customer retention strategy is essential for achieving these goals. This strategy should encompass personalized customer experiences, timely and proactive support, and a deep understanding of the customer's evolving needs.

Through regular communication and feedback collection, the customer success team can identify opportunities for improvement and tailor solutions to meet individual customer requirements. By prioritizing customer retention, the company can reduce customer churn, lower customer acquisition costs, and enhance its overall market reputation.

Chapter Two
The Customer-Centric Approach

The customer-centric approach is a business strategy that delivers an exceptional customer experience. This chapter will explore the techniques and metrics you need to know alongside real-world examples of implementing a customer-centric approach. You'll also discover how this strategy impacts upselling and cross-selling.

Why the Customer-Centric Approach Matters

A customer-centric approach is a business strategy that revolves around prioritizing the needs, preferences, and overall experience of customers. It involves placing the customer at the heart of all decision-making processes and aims to create exceptional value by understanding and fulfilling their expectations. This approach goes beyond just providing good customer service and requires a deep understanding of customer behavior, preferences, and pain points.

In a customer-centric organization, all departments collaborate to create a seamless and personalized customer journey. This involves streamlining processes, simplifying communication channels, and integrating customer feedback loops for continuous improvement. Building long-term customer relationships is a key focus that can be achieved by fostering trust, demonstrating empathy, and consistently delivering on promises. By cultivating strong long-term connections, businesses can enhance customer loyalty and retention, leading to increased CLV and a sustainable competitive advantage.

Implementing a customer-centric approach requires a shift in mindset and organizational culture. It involves aligning the entire company around a shared vision of customer success and embedding customer-centricity into core values and behaviors at all levels. Adopting technologies and tools that enable effective customer engagement, such as customer relationship management (CRM) systems, data analytics platforms, and customer feedback mechanisms, is also crucial.

Businesses can unlock numerous benefits when they embrace a customer-centric approach. Doing so enhances customer satisfaction and loyalty, as customers feel valued and understood. Satisfied customers are more likely to become brand advocates, referring others and generating positive word-of-mouth referrals. Moreover, it improves customer retention rates, reducing churn and the associated costs of acquiring new customers. Loyal customers are more likely to stick with a company over the long term, leading to stable revenue streams and sustainable growth.

A customer-centric approach also significantly impacts upselling and cross-selling. By deeply understanding customer needs and preferences, businesses can identify opportunities to offer additional products or services that complement the customer's existing portfolio. This personalized and consultative approach to upselling and cross-selling builds trust and makes customers feel like they are at the center of product decisions. This, in turn, increases the likelihood of customers being willing to expand their product usage and consider other offerings from your company.

Best Practices for Implementing a Customer-Centric Approach

- *Voice of the customer (VoC) programs:* To understand the customer's needs, it's crucial to gather feedback through surveys, interviews, and online reviews. This feedback can be used to identify areas for improvement.
- *Customer journey mapping:* Understanding the customer's journey can help identify touchpoints where the customer may have friction that is leading to dissatisfaction. By mapping the customer journey, companies can make data-driven decisions to improve the customer experience, personalize interactions, and ensure the customer's journey aligns with business goals.
- *Customer segmentation and personas:* Not all customers have the same needs, wants, and preferences. Segmentation and personas can help identify different types of customers and personalize their experiences.
- *Onboarding and implementation processes:* Providing a smooth onboarding process and implementing the product or service effectively can improve customer satisfaction and retention. (More on this in Chapter 12.)

Metrics to Measure

- *Net promoter score (NPS):* This metric measures the customer's likelihood of recommending the product or service to others, providing an overall indicator of customer satisfaction and loyalty.

- *Customer health score:* This metric evaluates the customer's likelihood of churning and their overall satisfaction with the product or service.
- *Churn analysis:* This metric evaluates the rate at which customers leave the company and identifies the root cause of the churn.
- *Customer success metrics and key performance indicators (KPIs):* These metrics evaluate the effectiveness of the customer success team and its impact on customer satisfaction and retention.

Real-World Examples

- *Apple:* Apple's customer-centric approach includes creating a seamless user experience across all devices, providing excellent customer service, and personalizing marketing campaigns.
- *Zappos:* Zappos' customer-centric approach includes offering free shipping and returns, exceptional customer service, and a 365-day return policy.

Why the Customer-Centric Approach Aids Customer Retention

By placing the customer at the center of all business decisions, companies can better understand their needs, wants, and preferences.

With this knowledge, they can improve satisfaction, loyalty, and retention.

Ultimately, this understanding can help companies provide a more personalized experience. Retaining existing customers is more cost-effective than acquiring new ones, leading to increased revenue and profitability.

How This Strategy Can Improve Upsell and Cross-Sell Opportunities

When a company takes the time to understand the unique path each customer follows, it can pinpoint instances where it's appropriate to present supplementary offerings that cater to their distinct demands.

Moreover, loyal customers who trust the brand tend to feel more inclined to explore and invest in other products or services it offers. Rooted in understanding and personalization, the customer-centric approach forms the bedrock of successful upselling and cross-selling endeavors.

Final Thoughts

A customer-centric approach is a retention strategy for any business that seeks to retain its customers and increase its revenue through upselling and cross-selling. By prioritizing the customer experience, companies can create long-term relationships, build brand loyalty, and, ultimately, grow their business. By focusing on the voice of the customer, the customer's unique journey, collecting feedback, and implementing customer segmentation and personas, companies can better understand their customers and provide them with personalized experiences.

Incorporating a customer-centric approach requires a shift in company culture and values, leadership commitment, and a dedicated customer success team that is focused on delivering customer-defined value and ensuring customer satisfaction.

Chapter Three
The Data-Driven Customer Retention Strategy

A data-driven retention strategy is a crucial approach that enterprise businesses use to optimize customer retention and enhance the overall customer experience.

By systematically collecting, analyzing, and utilizing customer data, this strategy helps teams make informed decisions and take targeted actions that foster customer loyalty and satisfaction. It involves gathering data from various sources, such as customer transactions, website interactions, social media engagement, and surveys. This data is then analyzed to extract meaningful insights and identify customer trends and preferences.

Utilizing predictive analytics, businesses can forecast customer behavior and potential churn risk, allowing for proactive retention efforts. Moreover, personalization based on customer data enhances satisfaction and builds stronger emotional connections with the brand, leading to increased loyalty. By embracing a data-driven retention strategy, enterprise businesses gain a competitive advantage, optimize operational efficiency, and drive revenue growth, all while focusing on meeting and exceeding customer needs and expectations.

This chapter delves into the significance of data-driven retention approaches and explores practical techniques, real-world examples, and metrics to measure success.

Why a Data-Driven Retention Strategy Matters

A data-driven retention strategy involves using customer data and insights to understand customer behavior, preferences, and pain points. When patterns and trends have been identified, enterprises can make informed decisions to tailor their customer success efforts and build stronger relationships with customers.

Data-driven retention strategies lead to enhanced customer satisfaction, increased loyalty, and reduced churn, all of which contribute to higher revenue and sustained business growth.

Best Practices for Implementing a Data-Driven Retention Strategy

- *Customer segmentation:* Categorize customers based on their characteristics, behaviors, and values to personalize interactions and support.
- *Customer health score:* Develop a customer health score that tracks KPIs to gauge customer satisfaction and identify at-risk customers.
- *Sentiment analysis:* Analyze customers' feedback and sentiment to understand their emotional experience with the product or service.
- *Predictive analytics:* Use predictive analytics to anticipate customer needs and offer proactive solutions before issues arise.

- *Personalization:* Use data insights to personalize communications, recommendations, and support for each customer.

Metrics to Measure

- *Customer churn rate:* Monitor the percentage of customers who discontinue their relationship with your company.
- *CLV:* Measure the total value a customer brings to the company during the entire course of their customer journey.
- *NPS:* Assess customer loyalty and the likelihood of a customer recommending the company to others.
- *Customer engagement:* Track customer interactions, usage patterns, and engagement with the product or service.

Real-World Examples

1. *Amazon:* Amazon leverages customer data to offer personalized product recommendations, resulting in increased customer satisfaction with its brand and shopping experience.
2. *Salesforce:* Salesforce uses predictive analytics to identify customers at risk of churn, enabling customer success teams to intervene and retain valuable customers.

Why a Data-Driven Strategy Aids Customer Retention

Data-driven retention strategies allow enterprises to better understand their customers' needs and preferences. By delivering personalized experiences and anticipating customer requirements, companies build trust and loyalty. This leads to increased customer satisfaction, reduced churn, and positive word-of-mouth referrals, contributing to a competitive advantage and long-term success in the market.

How a Data-Driven Retention Strategy Improves Upselling and Cross-Selling

When customer success teams understand their customers' evolving trends and habits, they can identify opportunities for upselling and cross-selling. Offering relevant products or services increases revenue per customer and maximizes the value of each relationship.

Understanding the Difference Between Data-Driven and Customer-Centric Approaches

A data-driven retention strategy and a customer-centric retention strategy are two distinct but complementary approaches to optimizing customer retention. While both aim to enhance customer satisfaction and loyalty, they differ in their core focus and methods.

A data-driven retention strategy primarily relies on the systematic collection and analysis of customer data to make informed decisions. It involves leveraging various data sources, such as customer interactions, purchase history, feedback, and behavior patterns. By using advanced analytics and machine learning algorithms, businesses can predict customer preferences, identify potential churn risks, and optimize retention efforts based on empirical evidence. The emphasis here is on data-driven insights to understand customer behavior and tailor retention tactics accordingly.

On the other hand, a customer-centric retention strategy centers around placing the customer at the heart of all business decisions and interactions. It requires a deep understanding of customer needs, preferences, and pain points. The focus is on building meaningful relationships with customers, actively listening to their feedback, and personalizing the customer experience to meet their individual requirements. This strategy involves fostering a culture of customer-centricity across the organization, ensuring that every team member is aligned on delivering exceptional customer service.

While data-driven retention relies heavily on quantitative data and analytics, a customer-centric approach emphasizes qualitative feedback and a deep understanding of customer emotions and motivations. Data-driven strategies excel at identifying trends and patterns, while customer-centric strategies are excellent for building emotional connections with customers and boosting customer satisfaction and loyalty.

Final Thoughts

Data-driven retention strategies empower customer success teams in enterprise companies to deliver exceptional customer experiences, build lasting relationships, and achieve remarkable business outcomes.

By leveraging customer data, segmenting customers, and employing predictive analytics, enterprises can enhance customer satisfaction, reduce churn, and drive significant revenue growth.

Embrace the power of data-driven retention to create a thriving customer success department that fosters customer loyalty and fuels your company's success.

Part II: Customer Understanding and Segmentation

"While a good leader sustains momentum, a great leader increases it by seeing opportunities others do not" — John C. Maxwell, *New York Times* bestselling author

Chapter Four
Voice of the Customer Programs

A voice of the customer (VoC) program represents a pivotal and strategic initiative for any forward-thinking business. It operates as a finely tuned mechanism designed to not just capture but profoundly comprehend the feedback, preferences, and ever-evolving needs of your customer base.

At its core, a VoC program is a systematic and meticulous approach to collecting, analyzing, and, most importantly, acting upon the invaluable insights provided by your customers.

In essence, it's a conduit that bridges the gap between your company and its most critical stakeholders: your customers. A VoC program goes beyond merely hearing what they have to say; it empowers you to truly listen, understand, and respond effectively. This proactive engagement establishes a dynamic feedback loop that continually refines your products and services in addition to the overall customer experience.

By systematically integrating customer feedback into your business processes, you're essentially leveraging a powerful compass that guides you toward customer-centricity. It enables your organization to pivot and adapt swiftly, ensuring that your strategies remain fine-tuned to meet and exceed customer expectations. Ultimately, a VoC program empowers you to place the customer at the very heart of your business operations, not only making it a cornerstone of improvement but sustainable success in today's competitive landscape.

Why Voice of the Customer Programs Matter

Here are some key reasons why a VoC program is crucial for your business:

- *Customer-centric decision-making:* By actively seeking and listening to your customers' feedback, you can make informed decisions that prioritize their needs and preferences. This customer-centric approach ensures that your business strategies are aligned with what your customers truly want, leading to increased customer satisfaction and loyalty.

- *Identify areas for improvement:* Customer feedback provides valuable insights into areas of your business that may need improvement. Whether your customers' pain points are product features, customer service processes, or the overall user experience, understanding them allows you to make necessary adjustments and enhance your offerings.

- *Enhance customer experience:* A VoC program enables you to identify the key touchpoints in your customer journey. By analyzing feedback at each stage, you can pinpoint areas where you can deliver exceptional experiences and stand out from your competitors.

- *Measure customer satisfaction:* Implementing metrics like net promoter score (NPS) and customer satisfaction (CSAT) surveys within the program allows you to quantify satisfaction levels. Tracking these metrics over time provides valuable data on customer sentiment and helps you gauge the effectiveness of your customer-centric initiatives.

- *Drive customer loyalty and retention:* Satisfied customers are more likely to remain loyal to your brand and continue doing business with you. By continuously improving your products and services based on customer feedback, you create a positive cycle of customer loyalty and retention.

- *Gain a competitive advantage:* Understanding your customer's needs and preferences better than your competitors gives you a significant advantage in the market. By leveraging customer insights, you can offer unique and tailored solutions that resonate with your target audience.

- *Build brand advocacy:* Happy customers become brand advocates. These people are more likely to recommend your products or services to others. Positive word-of-mouth referrals can drive new customer acquisition and organic growth for your business.

- *Foster a customer-centric culture:* A VoC program fosters a culture of customer-centricity within your organization. When employees at all levels of the company are encouraged to listen and respond to customer feedback, it creates a shared commitment to customer success.

Types of VoC Programs

- *Surveys:* Surveys are a common way to gather feedback from customers. They can be conducted via email, phone, or web-based platforms and can provide valuable insights into the customer experience.

- *Interviews*: Interviews, whether in person or over the phone, offer an avenue for acquiring comprehensive feedback from customers, shedding light on their first-hand experiences.

- *Online reviews:* Online reviews, such as those on Yelp or Google, can provide valuable feedback on the customer's experience with the company's product or service.

- *Social media:* Besides unlocking valuable insights into the customer experience, social media platforms such as X (formally Twitter) and Facebook can enable companies to engage with their customers and respond to their concerns.

Best Practices for Implementing VoC Programs

- *Define the objectives:* Before implementing a VoC program, companies should define their objectives. These might include improving customer satisfaction, identifying areas for improvement, and reducing customer churn.

- *Choose the right channels:* Companies should choose the right channels for gathering feedback based on their target audience and the type of feedback they want to collect.

- *Keep it simple:* Surveys and feedback forms should be short and straightforward, making it easy for customers to provide feedback.

- *Act on the feedback:* Companies should act on the feedback received through VoC programs, addressing areas of concern and making improvements to the customer experience.

Metrics to Measure

- *Response rates:* The response rate is the percentage of customers who respond to surveys or feedback requests. A higher response rate can indicate that customers are more engaged and willing to provide feedback.

- *Customer satisfaction score:* The CSAT score measures the customer's satisfaction with a particular product or service. This metric can provide insight into areas that need improvement.

- *Net promotor score:* The NPS measures how likely the customer is to recommend the product or service to others, providing an overall indicator of customer satisfaction and loyalty.

- *Customer effort score (CES):* The CES measures the ease of a customer's interaction with a company, product, or service. A lower score can indicate areas that need improvement in terms of customer experience.

- *Sentiment analysis:* Sentiment analysis uses natural language processing to analyze customer feedback and determine their sentiment toward a particular product, service, or experience. This can help identify areas for improvement and measure the effectiveness of improvements made.

Why VoC Programs Help Improve Customer Experience

Implementing a VoC program can help companies better understand their customers, including their needs, wants, and preferences. By gathering feedback and analyzing customer sentiment, companies can identify areas for improvement and make data-driven decisions to improve the customer experience. This can lead to higher customer satisfaction and loyalty, as customers feel that their feedback is being heard and acted upon.

How VoC Programs Can Improve Upselling and Cross-Selling Opportunities

A VoC program can impact your company's upselling and cross-selling efforts significantly. By gaining a deep understanding of your customer's needs, wants, and preferences, you unlock valuable insights that enable targeted and personalized upsell and cross-sell opportunities.

- *Tailored recommendations:* With a comprehensive understanding of your customers' preferences and pain points, you can make tailored product or service recommendations. By presenting offerings that align precisely with their needs, you increase the likelihood of successful upsells and cross-sells.
- *Personalized offers:* Armed with customer feedback, you can create personalized offers that resonate with individual customers. For example, if a customer recently purchased a

software product, the program can identify related features or add-ons that complement their current purchase, increasing the chances of an upsell.

- *Anticipate customer needs*: A VoC program helps you anticipate your customers' future needs and preferences. By identifying patterns in their feedback and behavior, you can proactively offer relevant products or services before they even realize they need them.

- *Building trust and loyalty:* When customers receive personalized offers that genuinely address their needs, it enhances their perception of your company. This level of care and attention builds trust and loyalty, making them more receptive to future upsell and cross-sell opportunities.

- *Enhancing customer lifetime value (CLV):* The strategy of identifying and fulfilling customer needs through upselling and cross-selling contributes to increasing CLV. Satisfied customers are more likely to stay loyal to your brand, engage in repeat purchases, and advocate for your products or services.

- *Creating long-term partnerships:* By consistently delivering relevant and valuable offerings, you foster long-term partnerships with your customers. These strong relationships lead to recurring business and referrals, further fueling your upselling and cross-selling success.

- *Data-driven decision-making:* A VoC program provides data and insights that guide your upselling and cross-selling strategies. By leveraging customer feedback and behavior data, you can make informed decisions and focus on high-potential opportunities.

- *Revenue growth and profitability:* Successfully executing upselling and cross-selling initiatives leads to increased revenue and profitability. As customers expand their engagement with your company, you maximize the value you derive from each customer relationship.

Final Thoughts

Implementing a VoC program is a crucial element of customer success for companies that want to improve their customer experience and increase revenue through upselling and cross-selling.

By gathering feedback and analyzing customer sentiment, companies can identify areas for improvement and make data-driven decisions to improve the customer experience. Response rates, customer satisfaction metrics, sentiment analysis, and other metrics can be used to measure the effectiveness of these programs.

Companies that successfully implement a VoC program can improve customer satisfaction and loyalty, increase revenue, and put their business on the path to success.

Chapter Five
Customer Journey Mapping

To effectively navigate the customer's experience and provide personalized support, customer success teams can leverage the power of customer journey mapping. By understanding the customer's perspective and optimizing touchpoints along their journey, organizations can foster stronger relationships, drive revenue growth, and achieve long-term success.

This chapter explores benefits, techniques, and real-world examples of implementing customer journey mapping within a customer success department. You'll also find key metrics for measuring the success of your mapping.

Customer journey mapping is a powerful tool that provides a holistic view of your customer's interactions with your company throughout their entire lifecycle. It helps you understand their experiences, pain points, and touchpoints across various stages, from initial awareness to post-purchase support. Visualizing this journey unlocks valuable insights into your customer's needs, expectations, and emotions, allowing you to identify areas for improvement and deliver a seamless customer-centric experience.

Why Customer Journey Mapping Matters

- *Enhanced customer experience:* By mapping out the customer journey, you gain a deeper understanding of your customers' experiences at each touchpoint. This knowledge empowers you to optimize each interaction, ensuring a consistent and delightful experience that fosters customer loyalty and satisfaction.

- *Identify pain points:* Customer journey mapping reveals potential pain points and roadblocks that customers encounter during their interactions with your business. This insight enables you to proactively address these issues, improving overall customer satisfaction and reducing churn.

- *Personalization opportunities:* Understanding your customers' preferences and behavior throughout their journey allows you to personalize your interactions and offerings. Tailoring your messaging and solutions to individual customer needs creates a stronger emotional connection, increasing the likelihood of repeat business.

- *Aligning business goals:* By aligning the customer journey with your business goals, you ensure that every customer touchpoint contributes to achieving your strategic objectives. This alignment enables your teams to work cohesively toward delivering exceptional customer experiences.

- *Decision-making support:* Customer journey mapping provides data-driven insights that support decision-making. It helps you prioritize areas that need improvement and allocate resources effectively to enhance the customer experience.

Creating a Customer Journey Map

Creating a customer journey map involves a structured process of gathering data, analyzing customer interactions, and visually representing the customer experience. Here's a step-by-step guide for creating an effective customer journey map for your business:

- *Define the customer persona:* Start by defining your customer personas, representing different segments of your target audience. Understand their demographics, preferences, needs, pain points, and goals. This information will serve as a foundation for mapping their journey.

- *Identify customer touchpoints:* Map out all the touchpoints where customers interact with your business, both online and offline. These touchpoints can include website visits, social media interactions, customer support calls, emails, in-store experiences, and more.

- *Gather customer data:* Collect data and feedback from various sources to understand how customers engage with your business at each touchpoint. Sources can include customer surveys, interviews, feedback forms, online reviews, and customer support logs.

- *Define customer journey stages:* Divide the customer journey into key stages, such as awareness, consideration, purchase, onboarding, usage, support, and loyalty. Each stage represents a distinct phase of the customer's experience.

- *Identify customer actions and emotions:* For each stage, identify the key actions that customers take and the emotions they may experience. Understand what drives their decisions and reactions.

- *Plot the customer journey:* Create a visual representation of the customer journey map using a timeline or a series of steps.

Plot the touchpoints, actions, and emotions at each stage, ensuring clarity and easy interpretation.

- *Validate with customer input:* Share the customer journey map with your team and, if possible, some of your customers. Validate the accuracy of the map by getting feedback and insights from both internal stakeholders and actual customers.

- *Analyze pain points and opportunities:* Analyze the journey map to identify pain points and areas of opportunity. Look for moments of friction, customer drop-offs, or instances where customers may feel frustrated or dissatisfied.

- *Optimize the journey:* Based on your analysis, prioritize improvements that will enhance the customer experience. Focus on removing pain points, optimizing key touchpoints, and personalizing interactions.

- *Implement changes and monitor:* Work with relevant teams to implement changes in the customer journey. Regularly monitor the impact of these changes on customer satisfaction and other key metrics.

- *Continuously update the journey map:* Keep the customer journey map dynamic and up to date. As your business evolves and customer preferences change, update the map to reflect the most current state of the customer experience.

Remember, customer journey mapping is an iterative process that requires collaboration between different departments within your organization. It provides valuable insights to help you create a customer-centric approach and deliver exceptional experiences that drive customer loyalty and business growth.

Metrics to Measure

- *Net promoter score:* Measure customer loyalty and satisfaction by gauging the likelihood of customers recommending your brand.
- *Customer effort score:* Evaluate the ease of customers' interactions throughout their journey, providing insights into areas requiring improvement.
- *Customer lifetime value:* Assess the long-term value of customers and their potential for upselling, cross-selling, and retention.
- *Customer churn rate:* Monitor the rate at which customers discontinue their relationship with your company, highlighting areas where improvements are needed.
- *Customer satisfaction:* Measure overall customer satisfaction at different touchpoints, identifying strengths and weaknesses in the customer journey.

Real-World Examples

- *Amazon:* Through customer journey mapping, Amazon optimized its e-commerce experience, providing personalized recommendations, easy checkout processes, and efficient customer support.
- *Airbnb:* Airbnb has improved the booking experience, leveraging user reviews and personalized recommendations to enhance customer satisfaction and trust.

- *Starbucks:* Starbucks utilizes customer journey mapping to deliver a consistent and seamless experience across their mobile app, physical stores, and loyalty program, resulting in increased customer loyalty and retention.

Why Customer Journey Mapping Aids Customer Retention

Customer journey mapping allows organizations to gain deep insights into their customers' experiences, pain points, and expectations. By understanding the customer's perspective, businesses can proactively address issues, tailor their offerings, and provide personalized support at every touchpoint. This level of attentiveness and customization leads to increased customer satisfaction, loyalty, and, ultimately, customer retention.

How This Strategy Can Improve Upsell and Cross-Sell Opportunities

Customer journey mapping enables customer success teams to understand preferences and needs at different touchpoints. They can use this knowledge to identify opportunities for upselling and cross-selling. By delivering targeted recommendations and relevant offers, organizations can increase revenue through upsells and cross-sells while simultaneously enhancing the customer experience.

Final Thoughts

Customer journey mapping is a strategic imperative for modern businesses seeking to excel in customer success. It empowers organizations to delve deeper into the intricate details of their customers' experiences, uncovering pain points and identifying opportunities for improvement. By visualizing the customer journey, businesses can align their strategies effectively, resulting in enhanced customer experiences, reduced churn rates, and increased customer loyalty.

This chapter has walked you through the importance of customer journey mapping, the steps to create an effective map, and the critical metrics to measure its success. Real-world examples from industry leaders like Amazon, Airbnb, and Starbucks have illustrated the tangible benefits of this approach.

Moreover, we've highlighted how customer journey mapping aids customer retention by allowing businesses to proactively address individual preferences and pain points. Additionally, this strategy facilitates upselling and cross-selling by enabling customer success teams to offer targeted recommendations and personalized support.

As you integrate customer journey mapping into your customer success arsenal, remember that it's an ongoing and collaborative process. Embrace the iterative nature of this practice, foster cross-functional collaboration, and stay attuned to your customers' evolving needs and expectations. By doing so, you'll not only drive customer satisfaction but also foster lasting customer relationships and sustainable business growth.

Chapter Six

Customer Feedback and Satisfaction Surveys

Customer feedback and satisfaction surveys are critical for understanding the customer experience and identifying areas for improvement. This chapter will explore the different types of customer feedback and satisfaction surveys, their benefits, and best practices for implementing them effectively.

Why Customer Feedback and Satisfaction Surveys Matter

- *Direct insights:* Surveys gather valuable opinions and insights directly from customers, helping businesses understand their experiences and satisfaction levels.
- *Sentiment analysis:* These tools reveal customer sentiments, pinpoint areas needing improvement, and assess the effectiveness of customer service efforts.
- *Deeper understanding:* Active feedback collection uncovers customer preferences, needs, and pain points — vital for delivering exceptional experiences.
- *Structured questions:* Surveys include well-crafted questions covering product quality, customer service, website usability, and brand perception.

- *Versatile channels:* Surveys can be conducted through various channels, such as email, online forms, or in-person interviews.

- *Informed decision-making:* Collected data informs business decisions, facilitates prompt issue resolution, enhances product features, and enables personalized customer experiences.

- *Performance benchmarking:* Surveys aid in benchmarking performance, comparing results over time, and setting improvement goals.

Types of Customer Feedback and Satisfaction Surveys

- *Transactional surveys:* These surveys are sent after a specific transaction or interaction, such as a purchase or customer service call. They can provide valuable feedback on the customer's experience during that interaction.

- *Periodic surveys:* These surveys are sent on a regular basis, such as monthly or quarterly, to gather feedback on the overall customer experience.

- *Relationship surveys:* A company might send these surveys to assess the overall relationship between the customer and the company. They can provide insight into long-term loyalty and satisfaction.

- *Customer effort score surveys:* These surveys measure the ease of a customer's interaction with a company, product, or service and can provide insight into areas that need improvement.

- *Net promoter score:* Turn to the next chapter for more details on NPS surveys.

Best Practices for Implementing Customer Feedback and Satisfaction Surveys

- *Define the objectives:* Companies should first define their objectives, such as improving customer satisfaction, identifying areas for improvement, or reducing customer churn.

- *Keep it short and simple:* Surveys should be short and straightforward, making it easy for customers to provide feedback and reducing the likelihood that they will stop part-way through the survey.

- *Choose the right channels:* Companies should choose the right channels for gathering feedback based on the customers they are surveying and the type of feedback they want to collect.

- *Act on the feedback:* Companies should act on the feedback received through surveys, addressing areas of concern and making improvements to the customer experience.

- *Communicate results:* Companies should communicate survey results to employees and stakeholders, demonstrating the company's commitment to improving the customer experience.

Sample of a Customer Feedback and Satisfaction Survey

Dear valued customer,

We greatly value your feedback and want to ensure that we are delivering the best possible experience for you. We kindly request a few moments of your time to complete this brief survey. Your responses will help us understand your needs better and enable us to make improvements to our products and services.

1. On a scale of 1–10, how satisfied are you with our products/services?

   (1 — Not at all satisfied, 10 — Extremely satisfied)

2. How likely are you to recommend our products/services to a friend or colleague?

   (1 — Not likely at all, 10 — Very likely)

3. Please rate your overall experience with our customer service team.

   (1 — Poor, 5 — Average, 10 — Excellent)

4. How often do you use our products/services?

   (Frequently, Occasionally, Rarely, Never)

5. What features or improvements would you like to see in our products/services?

6. Did our products/services meet your expectations? Please share your thoughts.

7. Have you encountered any issues or challenges while using our products/services? If yes, please describe them.

8. How do you prefer to receive support or assistance? (Choose all that apply.)

- Phone
- Email
- Live chat
- Self-help resources (FAQs, knowledge base, etc.)

9. Please rate the ease of use and navigation of our website/app. (1 — Difficult to use, 5 — Neutral, 10 — Very easy to use)

10. Would you like to share any additional comments or suggestions with us?

Thank you for your valuable time and feedback. Your responses are instrumental in helping us enhance our offerings and serve you better.

Sincerely,

Note: The questions above are just a sample, and the actual survey questions should be tailored to the specific needs and objectives of the business. Additionally, including open-ended questions can provide customers with an opportunity to share more detailed feedback and insights.

Metrics to Measure

- *Response rates:* The response rate is the percentage of customers who respond to surveys or feedback requests. A higher response rate can indicate that customers are more engaged and willing to provide feedback.

- *Customer satisfaction score:* This metric reveals the customer's satisfaction with a particular product or service. You can use it to get insights into areas that need improvement.

- *Net promoter score:* The NPS measures the customer's likelihood of recommending the product or service to others, providing an overall indicator of customer satisfaction and loyalty.

- *Customer effort score:* The CES measures the ease of a customer's interaction with a company, product, or service. A lower score can indicate that there are areas in the customer experience that need improving.

Real-World Examples

- *Amazon:* Amazon uses customer feedback surveys to gather customers' opinions on its products and services. The company also uses customer reviews to help other customers make informed purchasing decisions.

- *Delta Airlines:* Delta Airlines gathers customer feedback through surveys and social media to improve its customer experience and make data-driven decisions.

- *Zappos:* Zappos sends customer satisfaction surveys after each purchase, allowing customers to rate their experience and provide feedback on how the company can improve.

Why This Strategy Aids Customer Retention

Implementing customer feedback and satisfaction surveys can help companies better understand their customers and how happy they are with the company's products or services.

Gathering feedback and analyzing results allows businesses to identify areas for improvement and make data-driven decisions, ultimately enhancing the customer experience. This approach fosters higher customer satisfaction and loyalty, as customers recognize that their feedback is being heard and considered.

How This Strategy Can Improve Upsell and Cross-Sell Opportunities

The insights provided by a customer feedback and satisfaction survey can help companies identify opportunities for upselling and cross-selling. They unlock insights into the customer's needs, wants, and preferences, which can be used to offer additional products or services that meet their specific needs. This can lead to higher revenue and profitability, as customers are more likely to purchase additional products or services from the company.

Final Thoughts

Implementing customer feedback and satisfaction surveys is a crucial step for companies that want to improve their customer experience and increase revenue. They are indispensable tools for modern businesses, offering a direct line of communication with customers. This allows companies to build stronger relationships and make data-driven decisions that lead to better customer experiences and long-term success. By actively listening to their customers' voices, businesses can continuously evolve and stay competitive in an ever-changing market.

Chapter Seven
Net Promoter Score

Net promoter score, or NPS, is a customer satisfaction metric that measures the likelihood of customers recommending a company's product or service to others.

This chapter will explore the techniques involved with implementing NPS alongside key metrics to measure and real-world examples. It will also discuss its impact on customer retention and business growth.

How NPS Works

NPS was introduced by Fred Reichheld, a partner at Bain & Company, in a 2003 *Harvard Business Review* article. Since then, NPS has become a widely used tool for measuring customer satisfaction and loyalty across different industries.

The score is based on a simple question: "How likely are you to recommend this company/product/service to a friend or colleague?"

Customers are then asked to rate their likelihood of recommending on a scale of 0 to 10, with 0 being "not at all likely" and 10 being "extremely likely."

Based on their response, customers are then grouped into one of three categories:

- *Promoters:* Customers who respond with a 9 or 10. Promoters are loyal customers who are likely to recommend the company to others.
- *Passives:* Customers who respond with a 7 or 8. Passives are satisfied customers, but they are not as likely to recommend the company to others.
- *Detractors:* Customers who respond with a score of 0 to 6. Detractors are unhappy customers who may actively discourage others from using the company.

To calculate NPS, the percentage of detractors is subtracted from the percentage of promoters. The resulting score can range from −100 to 100, with a higher score indicating a greater level of customer loyalty and satisfaction.

Benefits of NPS

- *Easy to administer:* NPS surveys are simple and easy to administer, with just one question and a rating scale.
- *Actionable data:* The score provides actionable data that can be used to identify areas for improvement and make strategic business decisions.
- *Benchmarking:* NPS scores can be benchmarked against competitors and industry averages, providing a way to measure performance and identify opportunities for growth.
- *Predictive power:* NPS has been shown to be a reliable predictor of business growth and profitability, with higher scores correlating with increased revenue and customer retention.

Criticisms of NPS

Despite its popularity, NPS has also faced criticism from some researchers and practitioners.

- *Limited scope:* NPS only measures one aspect of customer satisfaction — the likelihood to recommend — and may not capture other important factors.
- *Lack of context:* The score does not provide any context for why customers may or may not recommend a company, product, or service, making it difficult to identify specific areas for improvement.
- *Reliance on averages:* NPS relies heavily on average scores, which can obscure important differences between individual customers or segments.

Real-World Examples

- *Apple:* Apple consistently ranks highly in NPS surveys, with a score of 72 in 2020. Apple uses NPS data to identify areas for improvement and make strategic business decisions.
- *Amazon:* Amazon uses NPS to track customer satisfaction across its many products and services, gaining a score of 62 in 2020.
- *Southwest Airlines:* Southwest Airlines has been using NPS since 2008, with a score of 80 in 2020. The company uses NPS data to drive continuous improvement and enhance the customer experience.

- *Tesla:* Tesla has a high NPS score of 96, which can be attributed to its focus on innovation, sustainability, and exceptional customer experience.

Why Calculating the NPS Aids Customer Retention

One of the most compelling functions of NPS scores and surveys is their ability to identify detractors and, in turn, guide them toward increased satisfaction and product loyalty.

Detractors are those customers who respond to the NPS survey with scores ranging from 0 to 6, indicating significant dissatisfaction with your product, service, or company. Identifying and addressing their concerns is not just crucial; it's an opportunity for significant improvement and retention.

NPS surveys provide a direct line of communication with detractors, shining a light on the specific pain points and issues they've encountered. By meticulously analyzing their feedback and understanding the root causes of their dissatisfaction, you can formulate a targeted approach to address these concerns. This can involve a variety of actions, such as improving product features, enhancing customer service, streamlining processes, or providing better documentation and support resources.

Furthermore, NPS allows for a closed-loop feedback system. This means that, upon receiving a low score, you can reach out to the detractor to gain deeper insights into their experience. Not only does this show that you genuinely care about their concerns — it also provides an opportunity to resolve their issues in a personalized and timely manner. Swift resolution can be a powerful tool for turning detractors into promoters because it demonstrates your commitment to customer satisfaction.

The insights gained from detractors can be a goldmine of information that guides product improvements and service enhancements. As you work to address customers' specific pain points and consistently deliver a better experience, you not only increase their satisfaction but also increase their likelihood of becoming loyal customers. When a previously dissatisfied customer witnesses the positive changes and improvements you've made based on their feedback, they are more likely to stick around and even become brand advocates.

Here's a summary of how NPS surveys can help with customer retention:

- *Identifying at-risk customers:* By identifying detractors, you can proactively address their concerns and work to improve their experience. Addressing issues promptly can help prevent churn and retain valuable customers.

- *Leveraging promoters:* Promoters are loyal customers who have the potential to become brand advocates. Engaging with them, encouraging referrals, and leveraging their positive experiences can attract new customers and improve retention.

- *Continuous improvement:* Regularly conducting NPS surveys allows you to track changes in customer sentiment over time. Consistently measuring NPS can help you monitor customer satisfaction and identify trends, allowing for continuous improvement in your products and services.

- *Insights for decision-making:* NPS feedback provides valuable insights into what customers love about your business and what needs improvement. You can leverage this data to make data-driven decisions that align with your customer's needs and preferences.

- *Benchmarking:* NPS scores can be benchmarked against industry standards and competitors, giving you a comparative assessment of customer loyalty and satisfaction. This helps you gauge your performance and identify areas where you can outperform competitors.

- *Tailored follow-up actions:* Based on NPS scores, you can design tailored follow-up actions for different customer segments. For example, you can send personalized offers to promoters or implement service recovery for detractors.

- *Retention strategies:* Armed with NPS data, you can develop targeted customer retention strategies. By addressing specific pain points and improving customer satisfaction, you increase the likelihood of retaining customers and building lasting relationships.

How NPS Can Improve Upselling and Cross-Selling Opportunities

Promoters are more likely to purchase additional products or services. By identifying these customers and targeting them with personalized offers and recommendations, companies can increase revenue and profitability.

Final Thoughts

The net promotor score stands as a powerful ally in the realm of customer satisfaction, loyalty, and retention. As businesses continually adapt to the ever-changing market dynamics, NPS provides a compass that guides them toward customer-centricity and sustainable growth.

By understanding how NPS works, its benefits, and real-world applications, companies can harness its predictive power to drive customer retention. Through NPS surveys, companies can identify at-risk customers, leverage promoters, initiate continuous improvement, and make informed, data-driven decisions to enhance the customer experience. Moreover, NPS facilitates benchmarking against industry standards and competitors, providing a holistic view of customer loyalty and satisfaction.

NPS isn't just a metric; it's a dynamic tool that empowers businesses to strengthen their relationships with customers. It not only measures customer satisfaction but also paves the way for increased customer acquisition, higher retention rates, and more fruitful upselling and cross-selling endeavors. To truly unlock the potential of NPS, businesses must foster a culture of continuous improvement, collaboration, and employee engagement.

In the ever-evolving landscape of customer success, NPS emerges as a steadfast companion, aiding businesses in not only understanding but also enhancing the experiences of their most valued asset: their customers. It's a metric that speaks volumes about a company's commitment to delivering exceptional value and forging lasting relationships in today's competitive market. As businesses continue to evolve, NPS remains a compass guiding them toward the pinnacle of customer-centric success.

Chapter Eight
Customer Health Score

A customer health score is a metric that evaluates the likelihood of a customer churning and their overall satisfaction with the product or service.

This chapter will explore the importance of the customer health score metric, how it's calculated, and its role in customer success. It will also provide examples of how companies use customer health scores to identify at-risk customers, prioritize their efforts, and improve customer satisfaction and retention.

Why a Customer Health Score Matters

A customer health score provides a holistic view of the customer's overall satisfaction with the product or service and their likelihood of churning. This metric helps customer success teams identify customers who may need additional attention and resources to improve their satisfaction. By tracking changes in the customer health score over time, companies can also identify trends and patterns that can inform their customer success strategy, product development, marketing campaigns, and sales strategies.

Let's consider an example of a software-as-a-service (SaaS) company that uses customer health scores. The customer health score is calculated based on various metrics that indicate how well the customer is adopting and utilizing the software, their level of engagement, and their overall satisfaction with the service.

In this example, the customer health score is measured on a scale of 0 to 100, where higher scores indicate a healthier customer and lower scores indicate a customer at risk. Let's say a customer, Company X, has a health score of 45, so it is considered to be at risk.

The low customer health score for Company X could be due to the following reasons:

- *Low usage:* Company X is not utilizing the software as frequently as expected. They are not taking advantage of the key features and functionalities that would help them derive maximum value from the product.

- *Lack of engagement:* Company X's users are not actively engaging with the platform. They are not logging in regularly, and their activity level is minimal, indicating a lack of interest or involvement with the software.

- *Unresolved issues:* Company X has raised several support tickets and reported issues, but they remain unresolved or have not been properly addressed. This indicates a lack of responsiveness from the customer support team, leading to frustration and dissatisfaction.

- *Declining satisfaction scores:* Company X has given low satisfaction scores in customer feedback surveys. They have expressed dissatisfaction with the product's performance, customer service, or overall experience.

- *Incomplete onboarding:* Company X's users did not receive a thorough onboarding process, resulting in a lack of understanding of the product's capabilities and how to use it effectively.

- *Non-renewal indications:* Company X has not shown interest in renewing their subscription or has expressed hesitations about continuing with the service.

Based on the low health score, the customer success team identifies Company X as a customer at risk. They promptly reach out to key stakeholders at Company X to understand their challenges and concerns. The customer success manager collaborates with the support team to resolve pending issues and provide additional training and resources to ensure that Company X gets the most value from the software.

The customer success team works closely with Company X to address the customer's specific needs, tailoring solutions to improve their experience and satisfaction. The goal is to increase their health score by ensuring they are more engaged, satisfied, and successful with the product.

By proactively identifying and addressing these issues, the customer success team can work toward improving Company X's health score and ultimately increase the likelihood of retaining the customer.

Calculating a Customer Health Score

A customer health score is typically calculated using a combination of factors, such as usage frequency, engagement with the product or service, support interactions, and customer feedback. These factors are weighted differently depending on the company's goals and objectives. For example, a company that prioritizes customer retention may place more weight on factors related to customer satisfaction and loyalty, while a company that focuses on revenue growth may place more weight on usage frequency and upsell/cross-sell opportunities.

Capturing customer data is essential for creating an accurate customer health score. There are several ways to capture customer data, including surveys, customer feedback forms, online reviews, and social media monitoring. These methods allow companies to gather data on customer satisfaction, sentiment, and overall health.

To create a health score algorithm that incorporates user data and customer sentiment, companies can follow these steps:

- *Define the variables:* Identify the variables that will be used to calculate the customer health score. These variables can include user engagement, user satisfaction, customer churn rate, and customer feedback.

- *Assign weights:* Assign weights to each variable based on their importance. For example, user engagement may be more critical than customer feedback, so it may have a higher weight.

- *Set thresholds:* Set thresholds for each variable to determine the health score. For example, if user engagement falls below a certain level, it may negatively impact the health score.

- *Analyze the data:* Collect and analyze the data from the various sources to calculate the health score. This may require a data analyst or software program to consolidate and process the data.

- *Incorporate customer sentiment:* To incorporate customer sentiment, companies can use sentiment analysis tools to analyze customer feedback, social media mentions, and other sources of sentiment data. This sentiment data can then be weighted and included in the health score algorithm.

Real-World Examples

- *HubSpot:* HubSpot's customer health score takes factors such as product usage, customer engagement, and support interactions into account. By regularly monitoring their customer health scores, HubSpot's customer success team can identify at-risk customers and provide targeted support to improve their satisfaction and retention.
- *Salesforce:* Salesforce's customer health score evaluates factors such as product adoption, usage patterns, and support interactions. By analyzing customer health scores, Salesforce's customer success team can identify trends and patterns that inform product development, marketing campaigns, and sales strategies.
- *Zendesk:* Zendesk's customer health score incorporates factors such as customer satisfaction, usage frequency, and support interactions. The customer success team can use customer health scores to prioritize their efforts and provide personalized support to those who may be at risk of churn.

Final Thoughts

A health score algorithm that incorporates user data and customer sentiment can be used to identify areas for improvement and personalize the customer experience, which ultimately improves customer retention and revenue.

By tracking changes in the customer health score over time, at-risk customers can be identified and provided with personalized support to improve their satisfaction.

Customer health scores can also inform strategic decisions such as product development, marketing campaigns, and sales strategies, leading to increased revenue and profitability. Incorporating customer health scores into the customer success strategy requires leadership commitment, a data-driven approach, and a customer success team focused on delivering value and ensuring customer satisfaction.

Chapter Nine
Customer Segmentation

Not all customers have the same needs, wants, and preferences, and segmenting them based on these factors can lead to better customer experiences. Customer segmentation is the process of dividing customers into groups based on their similarities and creating targeted strategies for each.

This chapter will explore the benefits of customer segmentation, the different types, and how to use segmentation in customer success departments to drive customer satisfaction and retention.

Why Customer Segmentation Matters

- *Personalization:* Segmenting customers allows companies to tailor their offerings, communication, and strategies to specific customer groups.
- *Cost-effectiveness:* Companies can optimize their resources and efforts by focusing on the most valuable customer segments, resulting in increased efficiency and return on investment (ROI).
- *Improved customer experience:* By identifying customer needs and preferences, companies can provide a more personalized and relevant experience, leading to increased customer satisfaction and loyalty.

Types of Customer Segmentation

- *Demographic segmentation:* Dividing customers based on demographic factors such as age, gender, income, and education.
- *Psychographic segmentation:* Dividing customers based on their personality, values, lifestyle, and interests.
- *Behavioral segmentation:* Dividing customers based on their purchasing behavior, product usage, and response to marketing campaigns.
- *Firmographic segmentation:* Dividing customers based on the size, industry, location, and revenue of their organization.

Using Segmentation in Customer Success

Here are some of the ways your business can get the most from segmentation and use it to improve customer success:

- *Identifying the most valuable customer segments:* By analyzing customer data and behavior, customer success teams can identify the most profitable and high-potential customer segments, allowing them to prioritize their efforts.
- *Creating targeted strategies and messaging:* Customer success teams can develop personalized strategies and messaging for each customer segment based on their unique needs and preferences.
- *Identifying upsell and cross-sell opportunities:* Customer success teams can identify opportunities to offer additional products

or services that meet the customer's specific needs when they understand their usage patterns and unique requirements.

- *Improving customer communication:* By segmenting customers based on their communication preferences, customer success teams can ensure that customers receive the right message at the right time and through their preferred channel.

Creating a Customer Segmentation Plan

- *Define customer segments:* Precisely defining your customer segments involves establishing clear criteria for each one. This can encompass a range of factors, including demographics (age, gender, location), behaviors (purchase history, engagement patterns), and specific needs or pain points. The goal is to create distinct categories that accurately represent the diversity within your customer base.

- *Collect customer data:* Gather relevant customer data to support your segmentation efforts. This data can be sourced from a variety of channels, such as surveys, feedback forms, purchase history, website analytics, social media interactions, and customer support logs. The more comprehensive and accurate your data collection, the more refined and meaningful your segments will be.

- *Analyze customer data:* With your data in hand, embark on a thorough analysis. Dive deep to uncover underlying patterns, behaviors, and preferences among your customers. This analytical phase is critical, as it forms the basis for segment creation. You'll be looking for commonalities, outliers, and key insights that will guide your segmentation strategy.

- *Create customer segments:* Based on your analysis, proceed to create customer segments. These segments should be well-defined, mutually exclusive, and collectively exhaustive, meaning every customer should fall into one segment. Segments may include categories like loyal customers, occasional shoppers, high-value customers, or customers with specific product preferences.

- *Develop targeted strategies:* Once your segments are in place, it's time to craft tailored strategies for each one. This step is all about personalization. Understand the unique needs, preferences, and pain points of each segment and use this knowledge to design strategies that resonate with them. These strategies might involve customized marketing campaigns, product recommendations, or support approaches, all geared toward maximizing engagement and satisfaction for each segment.

By following these comprehensive steps in creating your customer segmentation plan, you'll gain a deeper understanding of your customer base and position yourself to deliver highly targeted and effective strategies that enhance customer experiences and drive business growth.

Final Thoughts

Customer segmentation is an essential technique for customer success departments to understand their customers better and provide personalized experiences that lead to increased customer satisfaction and retention. By segmenting customers based on their needs, behaviors, and preferences, customer success teams can tailor their communication, education, and support to meet their specific needs.

The benefits are evident: personalization that resonates with individual customer groups, cost-effectiveness through resource optimization, and an overall improved customer experience that fosters satisfaction and loyalty. Furthermore, segmentation aids in identifying the most valuable customer segments, creating targeted strategies and messaging, spotting upsell and cross-sell opportunities, and enhancing customer communication.

In embracing customer segmentation, you're not only recognizing the diversity of your customer base but also embracing the boundless opportunities it presents. As you embark on your segmentation journey, remember that it's a dynamic process. Regularly revisit and refine your segments to ensure they remain aligned with your customers' evolving needs and preferences. By doing so, you'll continually elevate your customer success efforts and create a roadmap to enduring customer satisfaction and business prosperity.

Chapter Ten
Customer Personas

Customer personas, also known as buyer personas or customer profiles, are fictional representations of your ideal customers based on market research, customer data, and insights. They are detailed, semi-fictional characters that capture the characteristics, preferences, behaviors, and needs of different segments of your target audience.

Creating personas helps businesses gain a deeper understanding of their customers and enables them to tailor their marketing, product development, and customer success strategies to better meet their customers' needs.

Why Customer Personas Matter

By utilizing customer personas in your enterprise business, you can align your efforts with your customers' needs, create meaningful connections with them, and drive long-term customer success and loyalty.

Here's how you can use customer personas in your customer success strategies.

- *Targeted marketing:* Customer personas allow you to create targeted and personalized marketing campaigns. By understanding the specific needs and pain points of each persona, you can craft messages and content that resonate with them, increasing the chances of engaging and converting them into customers.

- *Product development:* Customer personas help inform product development decisions. By knowing what features and functionalities each persona values the most, you can prioritize product enhancements that align with their needs, ensuring your products are well-received in the market.

- *Customer success strategies:* Understanding your customers' personas allows you to design tailored customer success strategies. You can provide personalized onboarding, training, and support experiences, leading to higher customer satisfaction and retention.

- *Sales alignment:* Sales teams can use customer personas to better understand their prospects and tailor their sales pitches accordingly. This leads to more effective sales conversations and a higher likelihood of closing deals.

- *Customer communication:* Customer personas can guide your communication strategy. You can segment your customer base by personas and communicate with them through the channels they prefer, using language that resonates with their characteristics and preferences.

- *Identifying opportunities:* Customer personas help you identify new opportunities and untapped markets. By understanding different customer segments, you can explore new product lines, features, or services that align with their needs.

Best Practices for Creating Customer Personas

- *Collect data:* Gather data through surveys, interviews, customer feedback, and market research to understand your customers' demographics, behaviors, pain points, and goals.
- *Segmentation:* Group your customers into distinct segments based on similarities in their characteristics and preferences.
- *Persona creation:* Develop semi-fictional characters for each segment, giving them names, job titles, and personal details. Include information on their goals, challenges, buying behavior, and preferences.
- *Validation:* Validate your customer personas with data and insights from your sales, marketing, and customer success teams.
- *Implementation:* Share the customer personas with relevant teams across your organization and incorporate them into your marketing, product development, and customer success strategies.

Example of a Customer Persona

Customer Persona: Sarah Johnson

Background:

Sarah Johnson is a 35-year-old marketing manager working in a mid-sized cyber security company. She has been in her current role for five years and is responsible for leading the company's marketing campaigns and strategies. Sarah has a bachelor's degree in marketing and is highly skilled in digital marketing, social media, and content creation.

Demographics:

- Age: 35
- Gender: Female
- Location: San Francisco, California
- Education: Bachelor's degree in marketing

Job Role:

- Job title: Marketing Manager
- Company: CyberSecurity Inc.
- Industry: Information technology

Goals and Motivations:

- Increase brand visibility and market share for CyberSecurity Inc.
- Generate high-quality leads and drive customer acquisition through effective marketing campaigns.
- Build strong relationships with potential and existing customers.

Challenges:

- Facing stiff competition from rival companies in the tech industry.
- Balancing limited marketing resources with the need for effective campaigns.
- Navigating changes in marketing trends and technologies.

Preferred Communication Channels:

- Email: Sarah prefers email communication for official business matters and updates.
- LinkedIn: She actively uses LinkedIn for networking and industry updates.
- Webinars and industry events: Sarah attends webinars and industry events to stay updated on the latest trends.

Buying Behavior:

- Thorough researcher: Sarah conducts in-depth research before making any purchasing decisions. She reads online reviews, case studies, and testimonials.
- Data-driven: Sarah relies on data and analytics to assess the performance of marketing campaigns and tools.

Key Concerns:

- ROI and results: Sarah is focused on achieving measurable results from marketing efforts and demonstrating a positive ROI to the company's leadership.
- Quality and innovation: She seeks innovative marketing solutions that differentiate Tech Solutions Inc. from competitors.

How CyberEvents Inc. Can Serve Sarah:

- Tailored marketing campaigns: By providing data-driven marketing campaigns and personalized content, CyberEvents Inc. can cater to Sarah's need for measurable results and customer engagement by focusing on lead generation topics.

- Thought leadership content: Delivering high-quality, industry-specific thought leadership content can establish CyberEvents Inc. as a trusted source and help Sarah stay up to date with the latest marketing trends.
- Collaborative partnership: Building a strong relationship with Sarah through open communication and responsive support can enhance customer satisfaction and loyalty.

Creating customer personas like Sarah helps enterprises understand their customers on a deeper level, enabling them to offer personalized solutions, targeted marketing, and exceptional customer experiences. This approach fosters long-term customer loyalty and drives business success.

Using Customer Personas in Customer Success

- *Communication and engagement:* Using customer personas in customer success can help tailor communication and engagement strategies to the specific needs and preferences of each customer segment.
- *Product adoption and education:* Understanding different customer segments' needs and preferences can help inform product adoption and education strategies, leading to higher product usage and customer satisfaction.
- *Upselling and cross-selling:* Identifying opportunities for upselling and cross-selling based on different customer segments' needs and preferences can lead to increased revenue and customer loyalty.

Final Thoughts

A customer persona is a valuable tool for customer success departments in creating personalized experiences. By segmenting customers into personas based on their needs, wants, and behaviors, customer success teams can better understand their customers and tailor their approach to meet their specific needs.

Creating personas requires a deep understanding of the customer's demographic and psychographic characteristics, as well as their journey and pain points. This information can be gathered through a variety of methods, including surveys, interviews, and customer feedback.

Once created, customer personas can be used to guide the customer success team's interactions with customers, from onboarding to ongoing support. By understanding the unique needs and preferences of each persona, customer success teams can provide targeted solutions, anticipate future needs, and provide a better overall customer experience.

Customer personas can also be used to inform product development and marketing efforts. They can guide companies to develop products that meet their specific needs and create targeted marketing campaigns that resonate with them.

Overall, customer personas are an essential tool for customer success departments looking to improve customer satisfaction, retention, and revenue. By putting the customer at the center of all business decisions and using personas to tailor the customer experience, companies can build long-term relationships with their customers and drive business growth.

Chapter Eleven

Customer Acquisition Strategies: Balancing Growth and Retention

Customer acquisition strategies undoubtedly play a vital role in the growth and expansion of businesses by bringing in new customers and increasing revenue. They are essential for tapping into new markets, raising brand awareness, and gaining a competitive edge. However, as businesses focus on acquiring new customers, it is equally crucial to recognize the significance of customer retention for ensuring long-term success.

Balancing growth with retention is imperative for sustainable business development. While customer acquisition strategies bring in new customers, customer retention strategies focus on nurturing and retaining existing ones. Retaining loyal customers is not only more cost-effective than acquiring new ones but also contributes significantly to the bottom line. Loyal customers are more likely to make repeat purchases, recommend the brand to others, and provide valuable feedback for improvement.

Moreover, customer retention enhances brand reputation and fosters a positive customer experience. Satisfied and loyal customers become brand advocates, positively influencing potential new customers and promoting brand loyalty. By investing in customer retention efforts, businesses can build a strong and loyal customer base that provides a stable revenue stream and lays the foundation for future growth.

Ultimately, striking the right balance between customer acquisition and retention is a strategic imperative for businesses seeking long-term success. A holistic approach that combines both strategies ensures steady revenue growth, sustained customer loyalty, and a competitive advantage in the dynamic marketplace.

Types of Customer Acquisition Strategies

- *Inbound marketing:* Inbound marketing focuses on creating valuable content and experiences to attract and engage customers. This strategy includes tactics such as search engine optimization (SEO), content marketing, social media, and email marketing.

- *Outbound marketing:* Outbound marketing is a traditional approach that involves reaching out to potential customers through tactics such as cold calling, direct mail, and advertising.

- *Referral marketing:* Referral marketing involves incentivizing current customers to refer new customers. The effectiveness of this strategy relies on the trust and loyalty of existing customers.

- *Partnership marketing:* Partnership marketing involves collaborating with other businesses or organizations to reach a broader audience and attract new customers.

How Acquisition Strategies Impact Retention

Acquiring new customers is essential for business growth, but retaining existing customers is equally important.

Some customer acquisition strategies may lead to a high number of bad customers, which can negatively impact retention. Bad customers are those who are not a good fit for the business or product, have unrealistic expectations, or are difficult to work with. These customers can lead to increased churn rates and decreased customer satisfaction, ultimately affecting the company's bottom line.

Aligning the Business with the Right Customers

It's essential to align the business with the right type of customer. This involves understanding the target audience, their needs and preferences, and whether they align with the business's values and goals. By identifying the ideal customer profile, companies can tailor their acquisition strategies to attract the right type of customers and positively impact retention.

Real-World Example

Imagine that a SaaS company that provides project management software is looking to acquire new customers. They decide to run a promotional campaign that offers a significant discount to customers who sign up for a yearly subscription. As a result, they attract a customer who is primarily interested in the discounted price and doesn't fully understand the software's value.

This customer ends up being a bad fit for the product, as they don't have a large team to manage or complex projects to oversee. They also don't make use of the advanced features offered by the software. As a result, they end up being dissatisfied with the product and don't renew their subscription once the promotional period is over.

While the company did acquire a new customer through this promotion, this customer ultimately ended up reducing retention as they didn't align with the business or the product. Meanwhile, the company's resources were spent on acquiring a customer who didn't provide a positive ROI and ultimately churned.

In contrast, if the company had focused on acquiring customers who were a good fit for the product and had a high likelihood of renewing their subscription, they would have been more successful in the long run.

This example highlights the importance of customer acquisition strategies that prioritize acquiring the *right* customers rather than just focusing on increasing the *number* of customers.

Final Thoughts

Customer acquisition strategies are essential for business growth, but balancing growth with retention is important. Some strategies may lead to bad customers, negatively impacting retention rates. To avoid this, it's crucial to align the business with the right type of customers by understanding the target audience and their needs and preferences.

By identifying the ideal customer profile, companies can tailor their acquisition strategies to attract the right type of customers. Monitoring acquisition and retention rates over time and analyzing the cost per acquisition by channel can also help companies make data-driven decisions about their acquisition strategies.

Part III: Customer Success Strategies

"Customer satisfaction is worthless. Customer loyalty is priceless." — Jeffrey Gitomer, King of Sales

Chapter Twelve

The Importance of Onboarding and Implementation Processes

As an expert in customer success for enterprise companies, I have seen firsthand the crucial role that onboarding and implementation processes play in retaining customers and driving growth. In this chapter, we will discuss the importance of focusing on these processes, techniques to implement them effectively, metrics to measure their success, real-world examples, and how they can improve your upsell and cross-sell efforts.

Why Onboarding and Implementation Processes Matter

Onboarding and implementation processes are the foundation of customer success. They help customers understand the value of the product and how to use it effectively. By providing a seamless and positive experience, customer satisfaction and retention rates can be improved, leading to increased revenue and growth.

Unfortunately, customer onboarding is often overshadowed by other stages of the customer journey, such as marketing and sales efforts. When customer onboarding is overlooked or rushed, customers may struggle to adopt the product, leading to frustration, slow time-to-value, and even customer churn. In such cases, the company may miss out on valuable upselling or cross-selling opportunities.

A poorly executed onboarding process can leave customers feeling lost, confused, and unsupported, which may have the following consequences:

- *Lack of product understanding:* Customers may struggle to understand how to use the product or service effectively due to inadequate guidance during onboarding. As a result, they may not fully grasp the product's capabilities or how it can address their specific needs, leading to underutilization and dissatisfaction.

- *Slow time-to-value:* When onboarding is ineffective, customers may face delays in achieving the desired outcomes or benefits from the product. This slow time-to-value can lead to impatience and disappointment, as customers expect quicker results after investing in the solution.

- *Increased support requests:* Poor onboarding can lead to an influx of support requests from frustrated customers. This puts a strain on customer support teams and can create a negative perception of the company's responsiveness and ability to address customer needs promptly.

- *Churn and lost revenue:* Unsuccessful onboarding experiences can result in a higher churn rate, as dissatisfied customers may be more inclined to cancel their subscriptions or contracts. Lost customers mean lost revenue and missed opportunities for future upsells or cross-sells.

- *Negative word-of-mouth:* Customers who have a negative onboarding experience are more likely to share their frustrations with others, both in person and on social media.

Negative word-of-mouth can tarnish the company's reputation and deter potential new customers from engaging with the business.

- *Decreased customer loyalty:* A poor onboarding process can erode customer trust and confidence in the company. Customers may question the company's ability to deliver on its promises and be less inclined to continue their relationship with the business in the long term.

- *Missed upselling opportunities:* Without a successful onboarding experience, customers may not fully understand the additional value that can be gained through upselling or cross-selling. This can lead to missed opportunities to increase customer lifetime value (CLV) and revenue.

Investing time and resources in a comprehensive, personalized onboarding process can significantly impact customer satisfaction, retention, and advocacy, ultimately driving business success and growth. Thus, prioritizing customer onboarding is essential for building strong, mutually beneficial relationships with customers and maximizing the overall success of the customer journey.

Best Practices for Implementing Onboarding and Implementation Processes

- Develop a clear and comprehensive onboarding plan that outlines the customer journey and milestones.
- Assign a dedicated onboarding specialist to each customer to provide personalized support and guidance.

- Provide educational resources such as user guides, video tutorials, and webinars to help customers understand the product and its features.
- Conduct regular check-ins and assessments to ensure that customers are achieving their desired outcomes and addressing any issues.

Custom Onboarding

Custom onboarding is a personalized and tailored process designed to welcome and guide new customers as they begin their journey with a product or service. Unlike standard or generic onboarding approaches, custom onboarding takes into account the unique needs, goals, and challenges of each individual customer. It involves understanding the customer's specific requirements, preferences, and objectives and then designing a comprehensive onboarding plan that addresses them directly.

Through custom onboarding, companies can provide a more personalized and relevant experience, ensuring that customers feel supported, confident, and equipped to make the most of the product or service from the very start. This approach not only sets the foundation for a strong and productive customer relationship but also increases the likelihood of customer satisfaction, loyalty, and long-term success.

Metrics to Measure

- *Time to first value:* The time it takes for a customer to realize the full benefits of the product.
- *Adoption rate:* The percentage of customers who have adopted and are actively using the product.
- *Customer satisfaction score (CSAT):* The level of satisfaction that customers have with the onboarding and implementation processes.

Real-World Examples

Adobe

Adobe, a prominent software company, places significant importance on the onboarding and implementation process for its enterprise customers. Adobe's customer success teams collaborate closely with new customers to gain a deep understanding of their specific needs and creative objectives. They then craft personalized onboarding plans that guide customers through the configuration, customization, and integration of Adobe's creative and marketing solutions.

Adobe's onboarding process includes comprehensive training sessions, access to a vast knowledge base, and ongoing support to ensure a seamless transition. The company also employs key performance indicators (KPIs) and benchmarks to track each customer's progress during onboarding.

This meticulous approach not only accelerates time-to-value but also lays the foundation for long-term success. It empowers customers to maximize the full potential of Adobe's software, resulting in increased customer retention and revenue growth.

Zendesk

Similar to Adobe, Zendesk, a leading customer service software provider, recognizes the crucial role of onboarding and implementation in achieving customer success.

Zendesk's customer success teams work closely with customers to comprehend their unique customer support needs and challenges. They offer a structured onboarding process that encompasses software configuration to align with the customer's requirements, setting up ticketing and workflow processes and training the customer's support agents.

Throughout implementation, Zendesk establishes clear milestones and success criteria. The company routinely reviews progress with customers to ensure alignment with their objectives.

Zendesk harnesses analytics to monitor support ticket volumes, response times, and customer satisfaction scores. This data-driven approach empowers Zendesk to fine-tune its implementation strategies and provide proactive suggestions for optimizing support operations.

Zendesk's unwavering commitment to effective onboarding and implementation has enabled numerous customers to streamline their customer support processes, elevate customer satisfaction levels, and reduce resolution times. Consequently, customers are more inclined to renew their subscriptions, leading to enhanced customer retention rates and continued growth for Zendesk.

Why Onboarding and Implementation Processes Aid Customer Retention

Effective onboarding and implementation processes are cornerstones of customer success, playing a pivotal role in bolstering customer satisfaction, reducing churn rates, and boosting revenue. These processes are not mere introductions to products or services; they are personalized journeys that help customers realize the true value of their investments.

These processes bridge the understanding gap between customers' expectations and the actual benefits offered by the product or service. They provide tailored guidance and educational resources, ensuring that customers understand how the solution addresses their unique pain points and objectives. This clarity builds a strong foundation for customer satisfaction and a deeper commitment to the product.

Onboarding and implementation also act as churn-prevention measures. By proactively addressing customer questions and challenges early in their journey, onboarding and implementation reduce potential sources of frustration. Customers feel supported and empowered, diminishing the likelihood of seeking alternatives. Personalized support fosters trust, paving the way for long-lasting customer relationships.

How This Strategy Can Improve Upsell and Cross-Sells Opportunities

Effective onboarding and implementation empower customers to fully utilize the product or service. Customers gain the knowledge and skills necessary to extract maximum value, leading to increased engagement and usage. This, in turn, enhances customer lifetime value and opens opportunities for upselling and cross-selling.

Furthermore, by understanding the customer's goals and desired outcomes during the onboarding and implementation processes, customer success teams can identify opportunities to offer other solutions or upgrades. Offering additional features or services that align with the customer's goals enables the company to increase revenue and drive growth.

Final Thoughts

Onboarding and implementation processes are pivotal within the domain of customer success. They form the bedrock for achieving customer satisfaction, minimizing churn, and bolstering revenue. These processes extend beyond mere introductions, offering personalized journeys that empower customers to fully realize the value of their investments.

Their significance lies in bridging the gap between customer expectations and the actual product or service benefits. By tailoring guidance to address specific pain points and objectives, onboarding and implementation establish a strong foundation, nurturing not only customer satisfaction but also a deeper commitment to the product.

An onboarding program can act as an effective shield against churn by proactively resolving customer issues early on, which fosters trust and long-lasting relationships. By empowering customers to maximize product or service utility, these processes drive engagement, enhance customer lifetime value, and create upselling and cross-selling opportunities. In today's customer-centric landscape, prioritizing these processes is crucial for building enduring customer relationships and maximizing overall journey success.

Chapter Thirteen
High-Touch, Low-Touch, and Tech-Touch Strategies

In the realm of customer success for enterprise companies, the implementation of high-touch, low-touch, and tech-touch strategies can greatly enhance customer satisfaction, retention, and revenue growth. One of the key challenges for customer success teams is striking the right balance between high touch, low touch, and tech touch strategies to engage and support diverse customer segments effectively.

What are High-Touch, Low-Touch, and Tech-Touch Strategies?

High-touch interactions involve personalized and hands-on engagements with customers, providing dedicated attention to their specific needs and fostering strong relationships. This approach is well-suited to key accounts or high-value customers who require tailored solutions and ongoing guidance to achieve their strategic objectives.

At the other end of the spectrum, low-touch strategies leverage self-service resources and automation to empower customers to find answers to common queries independently. This scalable approach is ideal for customers with relatively straightforward needs or those who prefer a more hands-off approach to managing their accounts.

Tech touch, driven by technology and automation, strikes a middle ground between high and low touch. It enables customer success teams to efficiently engage with a broader customer base by leveraging digital channels, automated workflows, and knowledge bases to provide timely and relevant support. Tech touch is effective for delivering standardized information, guiding customers through onboarding processes, and addressing routine inquiries swiftly.

Why These Strategies Matter

A successful data-driven retention strategy combines the power of all three touch models, recognizing that different customers have varying preferences and requirements.

By adopting a hybrid approach, customer success teams can optimize resource allocation, providing the right level of attention to each customer segment. This enhances customer satisfaction because it enables businesses to meet the diverse needs of their customer base. The careful orchestration of these approaches ensures that each customer receives the appropriate level of support, resulting in greater customer success, higher retention rates, and sustainable business growth.

Implementing High-Touch, Low-Touch, and Tech-Touch Strategies

High Touch

a. *Assign dedicated customer success managers:* Identify key accounts or segments that require personalized attention and assign dedicated customer success managers to establish strong relationships, understand customer goals, and provide proactive support.

b. *Conduct regular check-ins:* Schedule regular meetings or calls with customers to address their challenges, gather feedback, and provide guidance on product usage and best practices.

c. *Offer personalized training and onboarding:* Provide tailored training sessions and onboarding programs to ensure customers smoothly and successfully implement your product or service.

d. *Establish a feedback loop:* Encourage open communication and actively seek feedback from customers to understand their evolving needs and continuously improve your offerings.

Low Touch

a. *Develop self-service resources:* Create a comprehensive knowledge base, FAQs, video tutorials, and online documentation to empower customers to find answers and solutions independently.

b. *Implement chatbots and live chat:* Integrate chatbots and live chat functionality on your website or within your product to provide instant assistance and address common customer queries. (More on this in Chapter 32.)

c. *Utilize automated onboarding:* Streamline the onboarding process through automated emails, product tours, and guided walkthroughs to help customers get started quickly and easily.

d. *Offer self-paced training programs:* Develop online training courses or webinars that customers can access at their convenience to deepen their product knowledge and skills.

Tech Touch

a. *Leverage targeted email campaigns:* Use marketing automation tools to send personalized emails to customers based on their behavior, milestones, or specific product usage patterns.

b. *Implement in-app messaging:* Utilize in-app messaging or notifications to deliver targeted messages, feature announcements, and tips directly within your product to drive engagement and adoption.

c. *Provide self-service analytics:* Offer customers access to their own performance metrics and data insights within your product, enabling them to track their progress and make data-driven decisions.

d. *Use customer segmentation:* Segment your customer base based on their usage patterns, preferences, or industry, and deliver targeted resources, updates, and offers to specific segments. (Go to Chapter 9 for more about customer segmentation.)

Metrics to Measure

- *Customer satisfaction score:* Measure customer satisfaction levels through post-interaction surveys to assess the effectiveness of high-touch, low-touch, and tech-touch interactions.
- *Net promoter score (NPS):* Serves as a valuable metric for assessing customer satisfaction and the effectiveness of the company's interactions with customers. This is because NPS measures the likelihood of customers recommending your product or service to others, reflecting their overall happiness with their experiences.
- *Time to value:* Track the time it takes for customers to achieve their desired outcomes or derive value from your product or service.
- *Adoption and engagement metrics:* Monitor key adoption and engagement metrics such as user activity, feature usage, and retention rates to evaluate the effectiveness of your strategies.
- *Renewal and expansion rates:* Measure the percentage of customers renewing their contracts or expanding their usage or subscription with your company. This indicates customer satisfaction and growth potential.

Real-World Examples

Let's consider a software-as-a-service (SaaS) company that offers project management solutions. The company separates customers into different segments based on their preference for high-touch, low-touch, or tech-touch interactions. Here's what the segmentation might look like:

High-Touch Segment

- *Example customer: A large enterprise with complex project management needs and a large user base.*
- *Characteristics:*
  - *High revenue potential:* The customer's substantial investment in the software makes them a high-value account.
  - *Complexity:* Due to the size and scope of their projects, they require personalized onboarding and ongoing support.
  - *Strategic importance:* The success of this customer can lead to positive word-of-mouth and attract other enterprise customers.

Tech-Touch Segment

- *Example customer:* A small-to-medium-sized business (SMB) looking for a cost-effective project management solution.
- *Characteristics:*
  - *Limited budget:* The customer prefers self-service resources and automated features to keep costs low.

o *Simplicity:* The customer's project management needs are relatively straightforward and can be met through standard features.

o *Scalability:* The software's ease of use and scalability align with the customer's growth plans.

Low-Touch Segment

- *Example customer:* A startup that needs a simple project management tool for a small team.
- *Characteristics:*

  o Self-sufficiency: The customer prefers minimal hand-holding and is comfortable exploring the software independently.

  o Limited resources: As a startup, the customer prioritizes budget constraints and time efficiency in managing projects.

  o Minimal intervention: The customer requires occasional guidance and access to self-help resources for a seamless experience.

By segmenting customers based on their specific needs, preferences, and project complexity, the customer success team can tailor their engagement strategies accordingly. High-touch customers may receive personalized onboarding sessions, regular check-ins, and dedicated account managers. Tech-touch customers can benefit from automated onboarding emails, chat support, and access to a comprehensive knowledge base. Meanwhile, low-touch customers might be offered periodic webinars, email newsletters, and a user-friendly interface for quick issue resolution.

Segmenting customers in this way allows the customer success team to allocate their resources efficiently and deliver exceptional value to each customer segment, ultimately leading to higher satisfaction, retention, and upsell opportunities.

Why High-Touch, Low-Touch, and Tech-Touch Strategies Aid Customer Retention

The combination of high-touch, low-touch, and tech-touch strategies caters to the diverse needs and preferences of customers, allowing them to choose the level of engagement that suits them best. Personalized interactions build trust and foster strong relationships, while self-service resources empower customers to find solutions independently. Targeted automation ensures timely and relevant communication, keeping customers informed and engaged. This comprehensive approach enhances customer satisfaction, reduces churn, and increases retention rates.

Final Thoughts

Utilizing a combination of high-touch, low-touch, and tech-touch strategies allows customer success teams to engage customers effectively, meet their diverse needs, and drive retention.

By providing personalized support, self-service resources, and targeted automation, you can enhance customer satisfaction, improve upselling and cross-selling opportunities, and drive business growth.

It is essential to continuously assess and measure the success of these strategies using relevant metrics to optimize and refine your approach over time.

Chapter Fourteen
Upselling and Cross-Selling

Client success teams are responsible for building strong relationships with customers, understanding their needs, and delivering value consistently over time — and part of this is recognizing and executing upsell and cross-sell opportunities.

In this chapter, we will explore techniques and strategies that an enterprise can implement to maximize its success in upselling and cross-selling, indicators that customers are ready to increase their spend, and metrics that can be used to report on the success of these strategies.

What Do We Mean by Upselling and Cross-Selling?

Upselling and cross-selling are sales strategies used to increase revenue from existing customers.

- *Upselling* is encouraging customers to upgrade or purchase a higher-tier version of the product they are interested in, offering additional features and benefits.
- *Cross-selling* involves offering complementary products or services that align with the customer's current purchase. For example, if a customer buys a laptop, cross-selling would be offering them a laptop bag or accessories.

Why Upselling and Cross-selling Matter

"Land and expand" is a business strategy where a company initially secures a small contract or engagement with a customer (the "land" phase) and then seeks to expand the relationship by offering additional products, services, or upgrades to that customer over time.

Implementing cross-selling and upselling in a "land and expand" approach is essential for a business's overall bottom line. It allows companies to maximize the lifetime value of each customer and increase revenue without incurring significant customer acquisition costs. By offering complementary products or upgrades, companies can leverage the trust and relationship already established with the customer, making them more receptive to additional offerings.

In the context of a SaaS business, cross-selling and upselling play a vital role in increasing a company's valuation. Investors and potential acquirers look at the average revenue per customer (ARPU) and customer retention rates as critical metrics for valuing a SaaS business. Cross-selling and upselling contribute to a higher ARPU by increasing the revenue generated from each customer.

Additionally, when customers see continuous value and benefit from upsells and additional offerings, their likelihood of renewing their contracts and remaining loyal to the SaaS company increases, resulting in improved customer retention rates. These factors positively impact the SaaS business's overall valuation, making it more attractive to investors and potential buyers.

Techniques and Strategies

One technique that customer success teams can use to upsell and cross-sell is to provide customized recommendations based on a deep understanding of their customer's needs. By understanding their customer's business objectives, pain points, and priorities, customer success teams can identify opportunities to sell additional products and services that will address these needs. Additionally, by providing ongoing value and building trust with their customers, customer success teams can increase the likelihood of customers purchasing additional products and services from the enterprise.

Another strategy is to leverage data and analytics to identify upsell and cross-sell opportunities. By analyzing customer usage patterns, behavior, and engagement with the enterprise's products and services, customer success teams can identify patterns that indicate a customer is ready to increase their spend.

For example, a customer who is using a product heavily or has recently adopted a new feature may be a good candidate for upselling or cross-selling. Another indicator is the customer's willingness to engage with the enterprise's customer success team. Customers who are regularly engaging with customer success teams are more likely to be receptive to upsell and cross-sell opportunities, as they are already invested in the relationship with the enterprise.

Metrics to Measure

- *Net promoter score:* This metric measures the likelihood of customers recommending the enterprise's products and services to others. An increase in NPS can indicate that customers are happy with their experience with the enterprise and are more likely to purchase additional products and services in the future.

- *Average revenue per customer:* ARPU is a metric used to calculate the average amount of revenue generated from each individual customer within a specific period. It provides insights into a company's financial performance by indicating the average contribution each customer makes to the overall revenue, helping assess the effectiveness of customer acquisition and retention strategies.

- *Customer lifetime value:* CLV measures the total revenue that a customer is expected to generate over their lifetime with the enterprise. By increasing CLV, enterprises can maximize the value of each customer and increase revenue.

Real-World Examples

- *Salesforce:* Salesforce's customer success team identified that customers were struggling to manage their customer data effectively. They created an upsell opportunity by introducing a new product, Data.com, to solve this. This resulted in an additional $300 million in revenue in 2013.

- *Dropbox:* Dropbox's customer success team identified that customers who were using the free version of the product were more likely to churn. To address this, they created an upsell opportunity by introducing a new product, Dropbox Business, which provided more storage and security features. This upsell strategy increased revenue and decreased churn.

- *HubSpot:* HubSpot observed that customers were struggling to generate leads. To solve this, the company created a new product, HubSpot Sales, which helped customers generate more leads and close more deals. This led to an additional $1.3 million in revenue in the first year.

- *Amazon:* Amazon's customer success team found that customers were interested in related products. They created a cross-sell opportunity by recommending related products to customers based on their purchase history. As a result, revenue and customer satisfaction increased.

- *Spotify:* Spotify's customer success team identified that customers were interested in attending live events. They created a cross-sell opportunity by partnering with event companies to offer tickets to concerts and festivals. This cross-sell strategy led to an increase in revenue and customer engagement.

Final Thoughts

Customer success teams play a critical role in upselling and cross-selling to an enterprise's current install base. By providing customized recommendations, leveraging data and analytics, and building strong relationships with customers, customer success teams can identify upsell and cross-sell opportunities and increase the likelihood of customers purchasing additional products and services from the enterprise. By using metrics such as NPS and CLV, enterprises can measure the success of their efforts and continue to refine their strategies over time.

Chapter Fifteen
Customer Loyalty Programs

Customer loyalty programs are a proven strategy for retaining customers. These programs encourage customers to continue doing business with a company and often provide incentives for doing so.

In this chapter, we will explore the techniques used in customer loyalty programs, the best metrics for measuring their success, and real-world examples of how these programs have helped companies retain their customers.

Why Customer Loyalty Programs Matter

Loyalty programs are a great way to incentivize customers to continue doing business with you. Not only do they help increase retention rates, but they also provide valuable data on customer behavior and preferences.

By offering rewards and incentives to loyal customers, businesses can build strong relationships that lead to long-term profitability. However, it's important to choose the right metrics to measure the effectiveness of a loyalty program and continuously refine the program to meet the evolving needs of customers.

Customer Loyalty Program Techniques

There are several techniques used in customer loyalty programs. Here are some of the most common:

- *Points-based systems:* Customers earn points for purchases or other actions, such as referring a friend or leaving a product review. These points can then be redeemed for rewards like discounts, free products, or exclusive experiences.
- *Tiered systems:* Customers are segmented into different tiers based on their level of engagement or spending. Each tier offers increasingly valuable rewards and perks.
- *Cash-back programs:* Customers earn cash back on their purchases, either as a percentage or a fixed dollar amount.
- *Rewards programs:* Customers earn rewards like points or discounts for making purchases or completing other actions.
- *VIP programs:* Customers who spend a certain amount or meet other requirements are given VIP status, which comes with perks like exclusive discounts, early access to products, and personalized service.
- *Referral programs:* Customers are incentivized to refer friends and family to the company, often with rewards for both the referrer and the new customer.
- *Anniversary programs:* Customers are rewarded for their loyalty over time, often with personalized offers or special discounts on their anniversary with the company.

Metrics to Measure

- *Points earned and redeemed:* This metric tracks the accumulation and redemption of loyalty points within a points-based system. It measures how actively customers engage with the program by earning points through purchases or other actions and subsequently using those points to claim rewards. A high rate of points earned and redeemed signifies strong program engagement and customer loyalty.

- *Tier advancement rate:* For tiered loyalty programs, this metric assesses how quickly customers progress through the tiers based on their level of engagement or spending. A high tier advancement rate suggests that customers are motivated to increase their engagement with the brand to access more valuable rewards and perks, indicating the tiered system has been successfully implemented.

- *Referral conversion rate:* In referral programs, this metric measures the percentage of referred customers who make a purchase or take the desired action. A high referral conversion rate indicates that the program effectively encourages customers to refer friends and family, contributing to customer acquisition and program success.

Real-World Examples

- *Starbucks Rewards:* This program allows customers to earn stars for purchases, which can be redeemed for free drinks and food. The program has been credited with helping Starbucks increase customer loyalty and drive revenue growth.

- *Amazon Prime:* While not strictly a loyalty program, Amazon Prime offers perks like free shipping and streaming of movies and TV shows to customers who pay an annual fee. This program has been successful in increasing customer loyalty and encouraging repeat purchases.

- *Sephora Beauty Insider:* Sephora's loyalty program rewards customers with points for purchases that can be redeemed for free products. The program has been successful in driving customer engagement and repeat purchases.

Why Customer Loyalty Programs Aid Customer Retention

The key to a successful loyalty program lies in providing incentives and rewards that encourage customers to stay loyal to the brand. By offering tangible benefits, such as discounts, exclusive access to products, or special experiences, companies can build emotional connections with their customers, boosting retention.

In addition, a well-designed loyalty program can provide valuable data insights into customer behavior and preferences, which can help inform future marketing and product strategies.

How This Strategy Can Improve Upsell and Cross-Sell Opportunities

Loyalty programs can also be an effective tool for driving upsell and cross-sell opportunities. By offering rewards that incentivize customers to spend more or try new products, companies can increase the lifetime value of each customer.

For example, a cosmetics company might offer a free gift with purchases for customers who spend over a certain amount, or a clothing retailer might offer discounts on new arrivals to customers who have made multiple purchases in the past.

By using data analytics to personalize these offers based on individual customer behavior and preferences, companies can further increase the effectiveness of their upsell and cross-sell efforts.

Final Thoughts

By implementing a well-designed loyalty program, companies can build stronger emotional connections with their customers, increase retention rates, and improve upsell and cross-sell opportunities.

However, it's important to keep in mind that loyalty programs are not a one-size-fits-all solution. To be effective, they must be tailored to each customer segment's unique needs and preferences and be regularly evaluated and updated based on data insights and customer feedback. With the right approach, a loyalty program can be a powerful tool for driving customer success and business growth.

Chapter Sixteen
Referral Programs

Referral programs can be a powerful tool in a customer success team's arsenal, allowing them to increase customer loyalty and satisfaction while also driving new customer acquisition.

In this chapter, we will explore the benefits of implementing a referral program in a customer success strategy, as well as the best practices to follow. You'll also find metrics that will enable you to measure the success of referral programs in addition to real-world examples.

Why Referral Programs Matter

In the realm of customer success for enterprise companies, the significance of referral programs cannot be overstated. These programs represent a potent asset for customer success teams, offering a dual advantage of enhancing customer loyalty and satisfaction while simultaneously facilitating new customer acquisition. At their core, referral programs are pivotal in augmenting the customer success strategy.

Referral programs matter because they operate as a strategic lever that empowers existing customers to become advocates and ambassadors for the brand. By incentivizing these satisfied customers to refer new business, customer success teams solidify the bonds of loyalty and satisfaction. Such referrals carry the weight of trust, as prospects are more likely to engage with a company that is recommended by a trusted associate.

Moreover, referral programs provide a low-cost, high-return marketing channel that complements and reinforces customer success efforts. By harnessing the goodwill of current customers, teams can tap into a network of potential customers who share similar pain points and needs, aligning perfectly with the company's solutions. This targeted approach not only reduces customer acquisition costs but also enhances the quality of leads.

Referral programs also contribute to enhancing customer lifetime value. Satisfied customers who actively refer others are more likely to remain engaged and loyal over an extended period. They become part of a community that fosters shared success and mutual support, reinforcing the brand's value proposition.

Best Practices for Executing a Referral Program

- *Define the program:* Determine the incentive structure, eligibility criteria, and rules for participating in the program.
- *Promote the program:* Develop a marketing plan to promote the program to existing customers and potential new customers.
- *Track and measure success:* Establish metrics for tracking the program's success and measure the impact of the program on customer retention, satisfaction, and acquisition.

Metrics to Measure

- *Referral conversion rate:* This metric calculates the percentage of referred leads or prospects who eventually become paying customers. A high referral conversion rate indicates that the program is effective in turning referrals into revenue-generating customers.

- *Customer retention rate:* Assess the impact of the referral program on customer retention by monitoring how referred customers compare to non-referred customers in terms of their likelihood of remaining with the company. An increase in customer retention among referred customers can be a sign of program success.

- *Referral velocity:* Referral velocity measures how quickly referrals are generated and converted into customers. A high referral velocity suggests that the program is creating a steady stream of new business opportunities.

- *Customer satisfaction score:* Gauge the satisfaction levels of both referrers and referred customers. A rise in CSAT scores for both groups indicates that the referral program is contributing positively to the overall customer experience.

- *Referral attribution:* Track the source of referrals to identify which channels or advocates are driving the most successful referrals. This helps refine your program's targeting and allocation of resources.

- *Customer lifetime value of referred customers:* Analyze the long-term value of referred customers compared to non-referred customers. If referred customers have a higher CLV, it demonstrates the program's impact on long-term revenue generation.

- *Referral program return on investment (ROI):* Calculate your referral program's ROI by measuring the revenue generated from referred customers against the costs associated with running the program. A positive ROI indicates the program is a financial success.

- *Referral program participation rate:* Monitor how many of your existing customers are actively participating in the referral program. A higher participation rate suggests stronger engagement and enthusiasm among your customer base.

- *Referral program advocacy score:* Create a scoring system that rates the level of advocacy and engagement of your referrers. This score can help identify your most influential advocates and encourage their continued participation.

- *Referral funnel conversion rates:* Break the referral process down into stages (e.g., referral submission, lead contact, conversion) and measure the conversion rates at each stage. This helps pinpoint potential bottlenecks in the referral journey.

Real-World Examples

- *Dropbox* increased sign-ups by 60% by offering additional storage space to customers in exchange for referring new users.

- *Uber* achieved a 25% increase in the number of rides per customer by incentivizing drivers to refer new drivers and riders.
- *Airbnb* successfully implemented a referral program in its customer success strategy, contributing to increased customer acquisition and retention.

Why Referral Programs Aid Customer Retention

Referral programs can be a powerful tool for retaining customers by increasing customer loyalty and satisfaction. Referrals from current customers can act as social proof, increasing the company's credibility along with that of its products or services. Additionally, referrals often come from satisfied customers who are more likely to remain loyal to the company.

How Referral Programs Can Improve Upsell and Cross-Sell Opportunities

Referral programs can significantly enhance upsell and cross-sell opportunities within a customer success strategy. By leveraging the power of referrals, companies can not only bolster customer acquisition and retention but also open doors to additional revenue streams.

Referrals often come from highly satisfied and engaged customers who have experienced the value and benefits of a product or service firsthand. These advocates, driven by their positive experiences, can be more receptive to upsell or cross-sell offers. Their trust in the brand, built through their referral experience, makes them more likely to consider and accept offers to expand their engagement with the company.

Via referrals, you can access a wider network of potential customers who may be interested in complementary products or services. When existing customers refer new prospects, they often highlight the broader ecosystem of offerings, paving the way for upsell and cross-sell conversations. This expanded reach increases the chances of identifying customers with specific needs that align with additional offerings, creating natural opportunities for upselling.

Additionally, referral programs can be strategically designed to include incentives for not only referring new customers but promoting upsell or cross-sell options, too. For example, customers who successfully refer others and those who accept upsell offers could receive special rewards or discounts. This approach encourages customers to actively participate in expanding their engagement with the company and its offerings.

Final Thoughts

To conclude this chapter, let me reiterate that referral programs stand as a cornerstone of successful customer success strategies. They offer a dual advantage of enhancing customer loyalty and satisfaction while simultaneously driving new customer acquisition. In terms of customer success for enterprise companies, these programs play a pivotal role in augmenting the overall strategy.

Referral programs transform satisfied customers into brand advocates and ambassadors, solidifying the bonds of loyalty and trust.

They provide a low-cost, high-return marketing channel that complements customer success efforts, reducing acquisition costs and enhancing lead quality. They also contribute to CLV, fostering a community of shared success and mutual support.

Best practices for executing a referral program involve defining the program, promoting it effectively, and tracking its success using various metrics. These metrics, such as referral conversion rate, customer retention rate, and referral program ROI, provide valuable insights into the program's impact on customer satisfaction, retention, and acquisition.

In essence, referral programs elevate the customer success strategy by fostering organic growth, driving customer loyalty, and optimizing the customer experience. They encapsulate the essence of customer success: creating a win-win scenario where delighted customers become enthusiastic advocates, all while expanding the customer base and nurturing long-lasting relationships.

Chapter Seventeen
Customer Education and Training Programs

I have seen time and time again how customer education and training programs are essential to achieving success and retaining customers. These programs not only help customers understand how to use the product or service effectively but also empower them to derive maximum value from it.

In this chapter, we will discuss how customer success teams can implement customer education and training programs in their strategy to achieve better results. We will cover best practices, metrics to measure, real-world examples, and the benefits of implementing this strategy.

Why Customer Education and Training Programs Matter

Implementing customer education and training programs is a powerful strategy for enhancing customer success and retention. By providing customers with the knowledge and skills to use a product or service effectively, companies empower them to achieve their desired outcomes and maximize the value they receive. Customer success managers (CSMs) play a pivotal role in these programs, as they can proactively identify areas where customers may benefit from additional education and support.

For instance, the CSM of a SaaS company that offers a complex analytics platform can identify customers who are not fully utilizing certain features and who may benefit from in-depth training sessions. Personalized training sessions enable the CSM to help the customers unlock the platform's full potential, leading to increased user satisfaction and retention.

Another example is in the case of a manufacturing equipment provider. The CSM of this company may notice that some customers encounter difficulties in maintaining the equipment, leading to operational disruptions. By offering hands-on training sessions and best practices for equipment maintenance, the CSM can empower customers to optimize their equipment's performance, resulting in improved efficiency and a higher likelihood of contract renewals.

Additionally, customer education and training programs can address broader industry trends or challenges. For instance, a financial services company's CSM might offer webinars and workshops on regulatory changes or emerging market trends. By providing valuable insights and expertise, they demonstrate the company's commitment to being a trusted partner and thought leader, fostering a sense of loyalty and enhancing customer retention.

Overall, customer education and training programs help build a stronger relationship between the company and its customers. By proactively addressing customer needs and investing in their success, CSMs can significantly impact customer retention and drive long-term loyalty. These programs demonstrate the company's dedication to their customers' growth and empower them to make the most of the products or services offered. This ultimately leads to improved customer satisfaction and a higher likelihood of continued partnership.

Best Practices for Implementing Customer Education and Training Programs

- *Develop comprehensive training programs:* Develop training programs that are tailored to each customer's unique needs. These programs can include webinars, training videos, e-books, and workshops.
- *Create an online knowledge base:* Creating an online knowledge base can help customers find answers to their questions quickly. The knowledge base should include product documentation, FAQs, and tutorials.
- *Conduct regular training sessions:* Conduct regular training sessions to ensure that customers are up to date with the latest features and updates. These sessions can be conducted in person or remotely via webinars.

Metrics to Measure

- *Adoption rate:* Measure the percentage of customers who have completed training programs or accessed the online knowledge base.
- *Customer satisfaction:* By measuring customer satisfaction against these programs, we gain valuable insights into whether they are producing the desired results and meeting the needs of our customers. High customer satisfaction indicates that the

training is effective, as satisfied customers are more likely to have a deeper understanding of the products or services.

- *Time to value:* Measure the time it takes for customers to realize the full value of the product or service after completing the training program.

Real-World Examples

- *HubSpot:* HubSpot Academy provides free online training and certification programs for customers to help them understand how to use the company's marketing, sales, and customer service software.
- *Salesforce:* Salesforce offers Trailhead, an online learning platform that provides interactive tutorials, courses, and quizzes to help customers learn how to use the company's software.

Why Customer Education and Training Programs Aid Customer Retention

Customer education and training programs demonstrate a company's commitment to helping its customers succeed. These programs empower customers to use the product or service effectively, resulting in higher satisfaction. Customers who understand how to use the product or service are more likely to continue using it, leading to increased customer retention and higher customer lifetime value.

How Customer Education and Training Programs Can Improve Upsell and Cross-Sell Opportunities

A well-designed customer education and training program can help customers understand the full range of features and capabilities the product or service offers. This knowledge can encourage customers to upgrade to higher-tier plans or purchase additional products, resulting in increased upsell and cross-sell revenue.

Final Thoughts

Implementing customer education and training programs as part of a customer success strategy is crucial for achieving better results and retaining customers. Tailoring training programs to each customer's unique needs, creating an online knowledge base, and conducting regular training sessions enables companies to empower customers to use their product or service effectively, resulting in higher satisfaction and retention rates. Additionally, this strategy can lead to increased upsell and cross-sell revenue by educating customers about the product or service's full range of features and capabilities.

Part IV: Building Customer Relationships

"The best way to find new customers is to take care of the ones you already have."
— Brian Halligan, CEO of HubSpot

Chapter Eighteen

Quarterly and Annual Business Reviews

Quarterly business reviews (QBRs) and annual business reviews (ABRs) are powerful tools that customer success teams can utilize to foster strong relationships with their customers. These structured meetings provide opportunities to assess progress, align goals, and strategize for the future.

This chapter explores the importance of QBRs and ABRs, techniques to implement them effectively, key metrics to measure their effect, real-world examples, and the impact these strategies have on customer retention, upselling, and cross-selling.

What are Quarterly Business Reviews and Annual Business Reviews?

QBRs and ABRs are structured meetings conducted by the customer success department with their key customers to assess the success of their partnership and plan for future collaboration.

- *Quarterly business reviews* take place every quarter, focusing on short-term objectives and performance metrics. During these meetings, the customer success team and customers review the progress made in the past three months, discuss any challenges faced, and strategize ways to achieve upcoming goals.

- *Annual business reviews* are held once a year and provide a more comprehensive overview of the entire year's performance. They delve into the achievements, challenges, and long-term objectives, shaping the strategic direction for the partnership.

Why Quarterly and Annual Business Reviews Matter

QBRs and ABRs are crucial for the customer success department's retention strategies for several reasons.

Firstly, these reviews enable relationships to be strengthened by showing the company's commitment to its customers and fostering a sense of trust and collaboration. By actively engaging with customers, listening to their feedback, and addressing concerns, the company demonstrates that it values the partnership.

Secondly, QBRs and ABRs offer a structured framework for performance evaluation. By measuring progress against predefined key performance indicators (KPIs) and goals, both parties can objectively assess the value delivered and identify areas for improvement. This data-driven approach allows for targeted problem-solving, addressing challenges promptly and minimizing the risk of customer churn.

Strategic alignment is another key benefit of QBRs and ABRs. By discussing long-term objectives and future plans, the company ensures that its offerings remain relevant to the customer's changing requirements. Not only does this alignment strengthen the partnership's foundation and contribute to mutual growth and success, but it also provides opportunities to identify upsell and cross-sell opportunities. The customer success team can offer additional products or services that solve the customer's pain points and align with their objectives, leading to increased revenue and customer satisfaction.

Ultimately, the regular engagement and goal-setting facilitated by QBRs and ABRs significantly improve customer satisfaction, leading to higher retention rates and an increased likelihood of contract renewals. By utilizing these reviews in their retention strategies, the customer success department demonstrates its commitment to providing value, fostering customer loyalty, and contributing to the company's long-term success.

Best Practices for Implementing QBRs and ABRs

- *Preparation:* Gather relevant customer data, usage metrics, and insights prior to the meeting. Understand the customer's goals, challenges, and desired outcomes.
- *Goal alignment:* Collaborate with the customer to review their objectives and identify areas where your solution can provide value. Discuss progress made and adjust strategies as needed.
- *Performance evaluation:* Evaluate the customer's use of your product or service. Highlight successes, address any concerns or roadblocks, and offer guidance on how to optimize usage.
- *Strategic planning:* Discuss upcoming product updates, roadmap enhancements, and future initiatives. Identify opportunities for collaboration and explore how your solution can support the customer's evolving needs.

- *Actionable recommendations:* Provide actionable recommendations based on data analysis and industry insights. Suggest specific actions the customer can take to maximize the value they derive from your solution.

Metrics to Measure

- *Customer satisfaction (CSAT):* Measure CSAT before and after QBRs/ABRs using surveys or feedback mechanisms. Track improvements in satisfaction levels over time.
- *Retention rate:* Monitor the retention rate of customers who participate in QBRs/ABRs compared to those who don't. Assess whether these reviews contribute to higher retention rates.
- *Upsell and cross-sell opportunities:* Track the number of upsell and cross-sell opportunities generated through QBRs/ABRs. Measure the conversion rate of these opportunities into actual sales.

Real-World Examples

- *Salesforce:* Salesforce conducts QBRs with its enterprise customers to review adoption, measure success, and identify expansion opportunities. These reviews enable Salesforce to strengthen its relationships with customers and drive ongoing value.
- *HubSpot:* HubSpot conducts ABRs to assess customer performance, review goals, and align strategies. These reviews

help HubSpot identify opportunities for upselling additional services and upgrading subscription plans.

Why Quarterly and Annual Business Reviews Aid Customer Retention

QBRs and ABRs play a pivotal role in maintaining strong customer relationships for several reasons. One key benefit is the opportunity they provide for fostering lasting connections. Regularly scheduled meetings illustrate your unwavering commitment to understanding your customer's objectives and helping them come to fruition. This establishes a foundation of trust, cooperation, and ongoing dialogue.

Equally importantly, these reviews offer a proactive platform for tackling any challenges or concerns the customer faces. By taking a preemptive approach to identifying and resolving issues, you underline your steadfast dedication to ensuring the customer's success.

These sessions also serve to reinforce the value your solution brings to your customer's business. Through showcasing the tangible impact, return on investment (ROI), and potential for future growth, you effectively strengthen their conviction in choosing to collaborate with your organization.

How QBRs and ABRs Can Improve Upsell and Cross-Sell Opportunities

Quarterly and annual reviews present valuable opportunities for capitalizing on upselling and cross-selling strategies. These reviews involve thorough conversations that allow you to delve into the customer's evolving needs, obstacles, and objectives. This comprehensive understanding serves as a foundation for recognizing additional products, features, or services that precisely align with their specific requirements.

Moreover, through these reviews, you're able to showcase the complete spectrum of your offerings and demonstrate how they effectively tackle the customer's pain points. This serves as a platform for emphasizing potential upsell and cross-sell opportunities since you present tailored solutions that directly address the customer's unique challenges and aspirations.

Final Thoughts

QBRs and ABRs are essential tools for customer success teams in enterprise companies. By implementing these structured meetings, organizations can strengthen customer relationships, align goals, drive value, and foster long-term success.

When customer success teams follow best practices, like solid preparation, goal alignment, performance evaluation, strategic planning, and offering actionable recommendations, they can maximize the impact of QBRs and ABRs. Key metrics such as customer satisfaction, retention rate, and upsell/cross-sell conversion rate help measure the impact and effectiveness of these reviews.

Real-world examples from companies like Salesforce and HubSpot demonstrate the value of incorporating QBRs and ABRs into the customer success strategy. By leveraging these practices, organizations can retain customers, identify growth opportunities, and build mutually beneficial partnerships.

Chapter Nineteen
Thought Leadership and Content Marketing

Client success teams in enterprise companies must go beyond traditional customer support and engage in strategic initiatives that drive value and build lasting customer relationships. One powerful strategy is the use of thought leadership and content marketing.

This chapter explores how customer success teams can leverage thought leadership and content marketing to enhance customer success, increase retention, and drive upsell and cross-sell opportunities. We will discuss best practices, metrics to measure, real-world examples, and the reasons why this strategy works in retaining customers.

What Do We Mean by Thought Leadership and Content Marketing?

Leveraging thought leadership and content marketing for customer success is of paramount importance for enterprise businesses.

- *Thought leadership involves establishing the company and its experts as industry authorities, sharing valuable insights, and offering innovative perspectives on relevant topics.*
- *Content marketing involves* creating and disseminating valuable content, such as articles, whitepapers, blogs, and videos, to attract, engage, and retain customers.

By employing these strategies, enterprise businesses can achieve several key benefits.

Why Thought Leadership and Content Marketing Matter

Thought leadership and content marketing showcase the company's expertise, credibility, and commitment to providing valuable solutions to customers' challenges. This positions the enterprise as a trusted partner and resource, building confidence and trust among existing and potential customers.

Such initiatives enable the company to proactively address customers' needs and pain points, as well as emerging trends across the sector. By providing valuable and relevant content tailored specifically to the challenges and intricacies of its customers' industries, the enterprise not only showcases its profound understanding but also actively cultivates a robust culture of customer-centricity. This commitment serves to enhance customer satisfaction and loyalty while solidifying the company's position as a trusted partner and go-to resource.

Moreover, thought leadership and content marketing serve as powerful tools for nurturing and maintaining long-term relationships with customers. By regularly sharing valuable insights and knowledge, the enterprise keeps customers engaged and informed, reinforcing their decision to partner with the company.

These strategies also contribute to lead generation and customer acquisition. High-quality content that resonates with the target audience can attract new prospects who are more likely to become customers if they perceive the company as a thought leader in its field. Furthermore, thought leadership and content marketing enable enterprises to stay ahead of the competition. By consistently producing and promoting unique, valuable, and informative content, the company can differentiate itself in the market and gain a competitive advantage.

Best Practices for Executing Thought Leadership and Content Marketing

- *Define your target audience:* Identify the key personas and segments within your customer base to tailor your thought leadership and content marketing efforts accordingly.
- *Develop a content strategy:* Create a comprehensive plan that includes topics, formats, channels, and distribution strategies to reach and engage your audience effectively.
- *Establish subject matter experts:* Identify individuals within your organization who can serve as thought leaders and provide valuable insights to your customers.
- *Create high-quality content:* Develop informative, relevant, and compelling content such as whitepapers, blog posts, videos, webinars, and case studies that address customer pain points and provide actionable solutions.
- *Engage through multiple channels:* Leverage various channels, including your website, social media, industry publications, and speaking engagements, to amplify your thought leadership and engage with your audience.

Metrics to Measure

- *Engagement metrics:* Track metrics such as website traffic, page views, time on page, social media shares, comments, and email open rates to gauge audience engagement.
- *Lead generation metrics:* Measure the number of leads generated through thought leadership content, such as form submissions, demo requests, or content downloads.
- *Conversion metrics:* Assess how thought leadership efforts contribute to upsell and cross-sell opportunities by monitoring conversion rates and revenue generated from thought leadership-driven leads.
- *Customer feedback:* Gather feedback from customers to understand the impact of thought leadership content on their perception of your brand and their decision-making process.

Real-World Examples

- *HubSpot:* HubSpot's blog and resource center offer valuable insights and actionable advice for marketers and sales professionals, positioning the company as a trusted thought leader in inbound marketing.
- *IBM:* IBM's thought leadership initiatives include whitepapers, research reports, and blogs written by experts that explore emerging technologies and their impact on industries, establishing the company as a leader in the technology space.

Why Thought Leadership and Content Marketing Aid Customer Retention

The effectiveness of this strategy in customer retention is deeply rooted in several pivotal elements. First and foremost, it serves as the bedrock for building credibility and trust — essential for maintaining lasting relationships with your customers. When consistently producing thought leadership content, your organization not only demonstrates its expertise but also nurtures an unwavering sense of trust among customers, firmly establishing your brand as a dependable and go-to resource in your industry.

Furthermore, this approach continually delivers ongoing value to your audience — a key driver of customer loyalty. Consistently sharing valuable insights and solutions tailored to your customers' needs means you can underline your dedication to their success and cultivate a sense of loyalty, ensuring they stay engaged and satisfied over time.

Thought leadership content also acts as a potent educational tool for your customers. Providing them with informative content about industry trends, best practices, and emerging opportunities empowers them to make informed decisions. This enhances their own success and reinforces their commitment to your brand.

Lastly, and importantly for customer retention, this strategy sets you apart from competitors. Thought leadership content enables you to spotlight your unique perspectives and innovative solutions, giving your organization a distinctive edge in the market. This distinctiveness not only helps attract new customers but also ensures that your existing customers remain loyal, knowing they are aligned with an industry leader that continually delivers value.

How This Strategy Can Improve Upsell and Cross-Sell Opportunities

The impact of this strategy on enhancing upsell and cross-sell potential is substantial.

When customers perceive your organization as a thought leader, they are more inclined to turn to you not only for the solutions you currently offer but also for additional products and services that might address other challenges they face. By consistently delivering content that addresses your customer's pain points and provides valuable insights, you create a natural pathway for identifying opportunities to upsell and cross-sell, all of which can be tailored precisely to meet their evolving needs and overcome various obstacles.

Furthermore, thought leadership's ability to showcase success stories and case studies plays a pivotal role. By demonstrating the tangible value your products or services have brought to other customers, you create a compelling incentive for your current customers to explore additional options, ultimately fostering their interest in expanding their engagement with your offerings.

Final Thoughts

Customer success teams in enterprise companies need to embrace thought leadership and content marketing as powerful strategies to drive customer success, retention, and revenue growth. By defining their target audience, creating high-quality content, and engaging customers through multiple channels, customer success teams can position themselves as industry experts and provide ongoing value to customers.

Measuring key metrics like engagement, lead generation, conversion, and customer feedback enables teams to gauge the effectiveness of their thought leadership efforts. Real-world examples from companies like HubSpot and IBM showcase how successful these techniques can be in building credibility, trust, and differentiation.

By integrating thought leadership and content marketing into the customer success strategy, enterprise companies can enhance their competitive advantage, retain satisfied customers, and unlock new revenue streams. With the right implementation and measurement, customer success teams can harness the power of thought leadership to drive long-term success and sustainable growth for both their customers and their organization.

Chapter Twenty

Public Speaking and Event Participation for Customer Success Managers

Public speaking and event participation are powerful tools for engaging and retaining customers. This chapter explores the benefits of these techniques, metrics to measure success, real-world examples, and the overall impact of leveraging public speaking and event participation to drive customer success, enhance customer retention, and boost upsell and cross-sell opportunities.

Why Public Speaking and Event Participation Matter

Utilizing public speaking and event participation is crucial for customer success managers (CSMs) as it presents numerous opportunities to foster strong customer relationships and showcase the company's expertise.

Public speaking engagements allow CSMs to engage with customers and prospects directly, demonstrating their knowledge, passion, and commitment to delivering exceptional service. By sharing insights, best practices, and success stories, they can establish the brand as an industry expert, gaining the audience's trust and confidence.

Additionally, public speaking offers a platform to address customer concerns, answer questions, and provide personalized solutions, further enhancing customer satisfaction.

Participating in industry events and conferences enables CSMs to network with potential customers, industry peers, and thought leaders, broadening their professional connections and opening doors to new business opportunities. The exposure gained from public speaking and event participation not only boosts the manager's credibility but also strengthens the company's brand reputation, positioning the organization as a valuable partner in the eyes of customers.

Ultimately, these efforts contribute to long-term customer success, increased retention rates, and continued business growth.

Best Practices for Public Speaking and Event Participation

- *Identify relevant speaking opportunities:* Research industry conferences, seminars, and events where your target audience gathers.
- *Develop compelling content:* Craft engaging presentations that highlight your expertise and that of your company. Offer industry insights and clearly set out your value proposition.
- *Deliver impactful presentations:* Practice public speaking skills, focus on storytelling, and deliver valuable content to captivate the audience.

- *Engage with attendees:* Actively participate in networking sessions, panel discussions, and Q&A sessions to build connections and gather feedback.
- *Leverage event promotion:* Use social media, email marketing, and other channels to promote your speaking engagements and generate interest.

Metrics to Measure

- *Event attendance:* Measure the number of attendees at speaking engagements and events.
- *Audience engagement:* Assess audience interaction, questions asked, and overall participation during presentations.
- *Lead generation:* Track the number of qualified leads generated through the events that the CSM participates in.
- *Feedback and testimonials:* Collect feedback from attendees and capture testimonials to gauge the impact of the CSM's presentations.

Real-Life Examples

Let's look at Salesforce as an example of how public speaking and event participation can be a useful strategy for customer success managers.

- *Context:* Salesforce, a leading customer relationship management (CRM) software company, hosts an annual event called Dreamforce, one of the largest technology conferences globally. At Dreamforce, Salesforce CSMs have a significant presence, utilizing public speaking and event participation to strengthen customer relationships and demonstrate expertise.

- *The role of CSMs:* Salesforce CSMs actively participate in Dreamforce by presenting in various sessions and panels related to customer success, CRM best practices, and industry trends. They also host dedicated customer success-focused sessions and workshops where they share insights and strategies for maximizing the value of Salesforce's products.

- *Engaging with customers and prospects:* During their speaking engagements, Salesforce CSMs engage with both existing customers and prospects. They share success stories that highlight how Salesforce solutions have helped businesses achieve their goals. They also address common pain points and challenges faced by customers, providing practical solutions and best practices.

- *Showcasing expertise:* By actively participating in Dreamforce, Salesforce CSMs showcase their deep knowledge of the CRM industry and Salesforce's products. They demonstrate their passion for helping customers succeed and their commitment to delivering exceptional service. This expertise resonates with the audience and establishes Salesforce as a trusted industry leader.

- *Networking and building connections:* Dreamforce brings together thousands of professionals from various industries. Salesforce CSMs leverage this opportunity to network with potential customers, industry peers, and thought leaders. They engage in meaningful conversations, offer advice, and build relationships that extend beyond the conference.

- *Strengthening brand reputation:* Salesforce's strong presence at Dreamforce enhances the company's brand reputation. Customers and prospects see Salesforce as a company that not only provides cutting-edge CRM solutions but also actively supports its customers' success. This perception positions Salesforce as a valuable partner in the eyes of its customers.

- *Long-term customer success:* The efforts of Salesforce CSMs at Dreamforce contribute to long-term customer success. Customers leave the conference with a deeper understanding of how to leverage Salesforce's products to achieve their business objectives. This knowledge leads to increased user adoption, higher customer satisfaction, and, ultimately, improved customer retention rates.

Why Public Speaking and Event Participation Aid Customer Retention

Involving customer success managers in public speaking and event participation holds significant potential for retaining customers, and there are several compelling reasons why this approach works effectively.

To start with, it's all about establishing credibility. When CSMs take to the stage as speakers, they position themselves as knowledgeable industry experts. This goes a long way in building trust and credibility with customers. Moreover, this strategy embodies thought leadership. Sharing valuable insights and expertise during presentations enables the customer success team to establish themselves as a dependable source of knowledge and guidance, effectively becoming a go-to resource for customers seeking advice.

However, it's not just about expertise — it's also about building strong relationships that will stand the test of time. Speaking engagements provide valuable opportunities for CSMs to connect directly with customers, reinforcing existing relationships and gaining a deeper understanding of their unique needs and challenges. These insights will enable the company to better serve its customers and keep them satisfied.

On a broader scale, this strategy contributes to brand visibility. By representing the company at industry events and conferences, CSMs increase the visibility and recognition of the brand among current customers and potential prospects. This exposure helps solidify the company's presence as a key player in the industry and reinforces the sense of partnership and collaboration with its customers.

How This Strategy Can Improve Upsell and Cross-Sell Opportunities

When CSMs actively participate in public speaking, it helps build robust relationships with customers, thereby creating an environment where customers are more open to considering upsell and cross-sell propositions. Moreover, through insightful presentations, CSMs can vividly demonstrate the value of supplementary products or services, showcasing the benefits of accepting upsell and cross-sell propositions.

Accessing decision-makers is critical to the success of upsell and cross-sell strategies. Events and speaking engagements put CSMs in the best place for interacting directly with key decision-makers, who are often the people who hold the authority to explore and invest in expanded solutions. Through personal interactions and engaging presentations, CSMs can effectively influence decision-makers, sparking their interest in exploring a broader range of offerings.

In essence, this strategy capitalizes on relationship-building, value demonstration, and targeted engagement with decision-makers to foster an environment ripe for successful upsell and cross-sell endeavors.

Final Thoughts

Public speaking and event participation are powerful tools for customer success managers in enterprise companies. By leveraging their expertise and sharing valuable insights with industry audiences, customer success teams can establish credibility, strengthen relationships, and retain customers.

Additionally, this strategy can improve upsell and cross-sell opportunities by building trust, demonstrating value, and providing access to key decision-makers.

By implementing the techniques outlined in this chapter and measuring key metrics, customer success teams can unlock the potential of public speaking and event participation to drive customer success and business growth.

Chapter Twenty-One
Partnerships and Alliances

Partnerships and alliances in customer success not only expand the company's capabilities but also strengthen customer relationships, ultimately contributing to increased customer loyalty and revenue retention.

This chapter explores the significance of partnerships and alliances, best practices to follow, metrics for measuring success, real-world examples, and the overall impact of utilizing these tools to drive customer success, enhance customer retention, and foster upsell and cross-sell opportunities.

Why Partnerships and Alliances Matter

Collaborating with strategic partners allows the company to offer customers a more comprehensive and diverse range of products or services, addressing a broader spectrum of their needs. By combining expertise, resources, and capabilities through partnerships, the company can deliver greater value and exceptional solutions, resulting in heightened customer satisfaction and loyalty. Additionally, these alliances can lead to cross-selling and upselling opportunities, as customers may be more inclined to explore new offerings from a trusted partner.

The sense of stability and reliability that comes with partnering with reputable organizations further solidifies the customer's trust in the company. Meanwhile, customer support and responsiveness can be improved, as the combined efforts of both parties can result in faster issue resolution and superior service delivery. As a result, customers are more likely to renew contracts and maintain long-term relationships with the company, driving revenue retention and fostering a sustainable business growth trajectory.

Best Practices for Leveraging Partnerships and Alliances

- *Identify strategic partners:* Research and identify companies or organizations whose products or services complement your own offerings.
- *Build strong relationships:* Cultivate relationships with potential partners through networking, industry events, and shared interests.
- *Collaborate on customer success initiatives:* Work with partners to develop joint success plans, share best practices, and align customer experiences.
- *Co-marketing and co-selling:* Collaborate on marketing campaigns, webinars, and events to reach a broader audience and generate leads.
- *Share customer insights:* Exchange customer data and insights with partners to create a more comprehensive understanding of your mutual customers' needs.

Metrics to Measure

- *Partner-generated revenue:* Measure the revenue generated through partnerships and alliances.

- *Customer retention rate:* Track the gross dollar retention (GDR) rate of customers retained through collaborative efforts with partners.

- *Upsell and cross-sell opportunities:* Monitor the number of upsell and cross-sell opportunities generated through partner collaborations.

- *Customer satisfaction:* Gather customer feedback to assess the impact of partnerships on their overall satisfaction. Look specifically at customers acquired or supported by partner relationships.

Real-World Examples

- *Adobe and Microsoft:* The partnership between Adobe and Microsoft integrates their respective technologies to provide a seamless experience for customers, leveraging shared resources and knowledge.

- *Cisco and IBM:* Cisco and IBM collaborated to develop integrated networking and cloud solutions. This partnership allowed them to provide end-to-end solutions for customers, enhancing their overall experience and increasing loyalty.

- *Amazon and Whole Foods:* Amazon's acquisition of Whole Foods resulted in a partnership that leveraged Amazon's e-commerce capabilities and Whole Foods' physical retail presence. This collaboration enabled seamless online ordering and delivery, enhancing convenience for customers and driving cross-selling opportunities.

Why Partnerships and Alliances Aid Customer Retention

Partnerships and alliances play a pivotal role in bolstering customer retention through several key mechanisms. Firstly, these collaborations enable customer success teams to provide customers with comprehensive solutions that draw upon the combined expertise of both their own organization and their partners. This synergy allows for a more holistic approach to addressing customer needs and challenges.

Additionally, partnering with other organizations grants access to specialized resources and capabilities that might otherwise be unavailable. These resources can be particularly valuable when addressing unique and complex customer requirements, enhancing the overall value proposition.

Forming partnerships with reputable companies significantly expands a brand's reach and enhances its credibility. This expansion not only attracts new customers but also instills confidence in existing ones, reaffirming their loyalty to the brand.

Perhaps most importantly, these alliances foster a shared customer success focus. By aligning goals and strategies with partners, customer success teams can work collaboratively toward the common objective of delivering exceptional customer experiences.

This cooperative approach not only strengthens relationships but also ensures that customers receive the highest level of support and satisfaction possible.

How This Strategy Can Improve Upsell and Cross-Sell Opportunities

Prioritizing partnerships and alliances can significantly enhance opportunities for upselling and cross-selling. This strategy facilitates the expansion of your product and service offerings by enabling your customer success teams to provide a broader range of solutions to your existing customers.

This approach also opens up access to entirely new customer segments, granting you entry into previously untapped markets and extending the scope of potential customers who can benefit from your upselling and cross-selling efforts.

Additionally, the strategy leverages the combined expertise of your organization and your partners, allowing for more precise and effective upsell and cross-sell recommendations. With a deeper understanding of your customers' needs, you can tailor your offerings to address their specific pain points, increasing the likelihood of successful upsell and cross-sell initiatives.

Final Thoughts

Partnerships and alliances offer valuable opportunities for customer success teams in enterprise companies to enhance customer success, retention, and upsell and cross-sell efforts.

Through techniques such as identifying strategic partners, fostering strong relationships, collaborating on customer success initiatives, and sharing insights, customer success teams can unlock the benefits of partnerships. Meanwhile, measuring metrics such as partner-generated revenue, customer retention rate, upsell and cross-sell opportunities, and customer satisfaction enables teams to track the impact of their partnership strategies.

Ultimately, by leveraging partnerships and alliances, customer success teams can provide comprehensive solutions, access specialized resources, expand their reach and credibility, and align their focus with partners to drive customer success.

Chapter Twenty-Two
Customer Advisory Boards

This chapter explores the valuable role of customer advisory boards (CABs) in driving customer success for enterprise companies. CABs are strategic forums comprised of select customers who provide insights, feedback, and guidance to help shape the organization's direction. By leveraging CABs, customer success teams can tap into the collective wisdom of their most influential customers, fostering strong relationships, enhancing product and service offerings, and, ultimately, retaining and expanding their customer base.

What is a Customer Advisory Board?

A customer advisory board is a select group of key customers or customers from various industries who come together to provide valuable feedback, insights, and suggestions to a company. These individuals are typically considered industry experts or thought leaders, and their role is to act as strategic advisors, offering perspectives on the company's products, services, and overall business strategy.

The board members meet regularly, either in person or virtually, to discuss their experiences, challenges, and needs, enabling the company to gain a deeper understanding of its customers and tailor its offerings to better meet their requirements.

There are costs involved with hosting a CAB. The company needs to allocate resources to organize and manage board meetings, including logistics, technology, and administrative support. Travel and accommodation expenses may be incurred if in-person meetings are conducted. Moreover, compensating advisory board members for their time and expertise may be necessary to ensure their active and sustained participation.

Why Customer Advisory Boards Matter

Offering a customer advisory board has several benefits. Firstly, it creates a direct channel of communication between the company and its most valuable customers, fostering a strong sense of partnership and mutual trust. By actively involving customers in the decision-making process, the company demonstrates its commitment to customer-centricity and responsiveness, enhancing customer satisfaction and loyalty.

Additionally, the insights and feedback gained from the advisory board offer the company invaluable market intelligence, helping to identify emerging trends, address potential issues, and stay ahead of competitors. The board's diverse perspectives can also lead to innovative product or service ideas and improvements, ultimately driving business growth and revenue.

Despite the costs involved with customer advisory boards, the value gained from the insights strengthens customer relationships. The competitive advantages resulting from a CAB often outweigh the financial investments involved, making it a worthwhile strategy for businesses looking to enhance customer success and long-term profitability.

Best Practices for Implementing Customer Advisory Boards

- *Establishing the CAB:* Identify key customers who exhibit deep product knowledge, engagement, and a willingness to collaborate. Invite them to join the CAB and define its purpose, structure, and expected time commitment.

- *Structured meetings:* Plan and facilitate regular CAB meetings, either in person or virtually, to discuss strategic initiatives and product roadmaps and gather customer insights. Provide an agenda in advance and ensure active participation from both the customer success team and CAB members.

- *Collaborative feedback:* Encourage open and honest discussions where CAB members can provide feedback, share challenges, and suggest improvements. Leverage this input to inform strategic decision-making and shape the organization's customer success initiatives.

- *Actionable recommendations:* Transform CAB insights into actionable recommendations that align with customer needs and expectations. Implement changes based on CAB feedback and communicate the outcomes to demonstrate the value of their input.

Metrics to Measure

- *CAB engagement:* Track CAB member participation and contribution in meetings, surveys, and working groups.

Measure attendance rates, active involvement, and the quality of insights shared.

- *Customer satisfaction:* Monitor customer satisfaction metrics such as net promoter score (NPS) or CSAT among CAB members and the wider customer base. Compare CAB members' satisfaction levels with those of non-CAB members to assess the program's impact.

- *Product enhancement:* Evaluate the number of product enhancements or features implemented based on CAB recommendations. Measure the success and adoption rate of these enhancements to determine their effectiveness.

Real-World Examples

- *Microsoft:* Microsoft operates the Microsoft Customer Advisory Board (MCAB), which comprises influential customers who provide feedback and strategic guidance on Microsoft products and services. The MCAB allows Microsoft to align its offerings with customer needs and drive continuous improvement.

- *Salesforce:* Salesforce hosts the Salesforce Customer Advisory Board (CAB) program, where select customers collaborate with Salesforce executives to shape the company's product roadmap, provide feedback, and share best practices. This engagement helps Salesforce enhance customer success and drives innovation within its platform.

Why Customer Advisory Boards Aid Customer Retention

Customer advisory boards play a crucial role in aiding customer retention through several key mechanisms. Firstly, they foster a collaborative relationship by actively involving customers in strategic discussions and decision-making processes. This engagement strengthens the bond between customers and the organization, clearly demonstrating a commitment to their success.

Secondly, CABs ensure a customer-centric approach by directly capturing valuable insights and feedback from influential customers. This approach allows organizations to gain a deeper understanding of customer needs and expectations, enabling them to align their strategies, products, and services more effectively.

Participation in CABs also instills a sense of ownership among participants. Involving these customers in shaping the company's future direction enables them to develop a strong sense of advocacy and loyalty. This, in turn, contributes to increased customer retention rates and a reduction in churn, as these individuals become steadfast supporters of the organization's success.

How CABs Can Improve Upsell and Cross-Sell Opportunities

Customer advisory boards offer various avenues for improving upsell and cross-sell opportunities. Identifying expansion opportunities is a key part of this. CAB members, known for their high engagement levels, tend to offer valuable insights into potential areas for expansion or the introduction of new products.

CAB members are often early adopters of new features or products. Their positive experiences and advocacy can significantly influence other customers, prompting them to explore additional offerings. When CAB members share customer success stories, this has a substantial influence.

Lastly, through close collaboration with CAB members, customer success teams can gain a deeper understanding of individual customer needs and preferences. This invaluable insight enables the customer success team to recommend additional products or services that are highly relevant to each customer.

Final Thoughts

Incorporating customer advisory boards into customer success strategies empowers enterprise companies to leverage the expertise and insights of their most influential customers. By engaging with CAB members, organizations can enhance their understanding of customer needs, align their strategies and offerings accordingly, and build strong, long-term relationships.

The CAB program not only contributes to customer retention but also presents opportunities for upselling and cross-selling, ultimately driving revenue growth. By implementing the techniques outlined in this chapter and leveraging the metrics for measurement, customer success teams can establish successful CAB initiatives that result in customer loyalty, product innovation, and business success.

Chapter Twenty-Three
Industry Research and Benchmarking

Client success teams in enterprise companies should leverage industry research and benchmarking to succeed in their role and drive retention and revenue. In this chapter, we'll dive into why industry research and benchmarking are so important for customer success, best practices, metrics to measure the success of your efforts, real-world examples from leading companies, and how this strategy can improve upsell and cross-sell opportunities.

Why Industry Research and Benchmarking Matter

A customer success department should engage in industry research and benchmarking to support customers for several compelling reasons.

Firstly, industry research allows the department to stay abreast of the latest trends, developments, and challenges within customers' respective sectors. By understanding the broader industry landscape, the team can provide customers with valuable insights and recommendations tailored to their specific needs and goals. This knowledge empowers customer success managers to proactively address emerging issues and anticipate potential opportunities, ensuring that customers receive relevant and timely guidance.

Secondly, benchmarking against industry standards and best practices enables the team to measure a customer's performance and progress relative to their peers. If areas are identified where customers are excelling or lagging behind, the team can work with them collaboratively to develop strategies for improvement and optimization. This process also helps set realistic goals and expectations, contributing to customer success and satisfaction.

Moreover, industry research and benchmarking can lead to the discovery of innovative solutions or ideas from other successful companies in the same sector. Leveraging these insights enables the customer success department to offer customers cutting-edge strategies and approaches that will position them as forward-thinking and competitive players in their industries.

Additionally, customers often appreciate working with a customer success team that demonstrates in-depth knowledge and expertise in their specific field. Industry research and benchmarking enable the department to build credibility and trust with customers, further solidifying partnerships and fostering long-term loyalty.

Best Practices for Using Industry Research and Benchmarking

- *Stay informed:* Customer success teams should actively keep up to date on industry trends, market insights, and best practices. This can be achieved by continuously monitoring industry publications and research reports and attending relevant conferences and webinars.

- *Regular benchmarking:* Conduct regular benchmarking exercises to compare your customers' adoption and performance against industry standards. Identify areas that need improvement and set goals to align with or surpass industry benchmarks.

- *Collaborate with industry experts:* Foster relationships with industry thought leaders, consultants, and analysts who can provide valuable insights and guidance. Engage in discussions, attend workshops, and seek their expertise to gain a deeper understanding of industry dynamics.

Metrics to Measure

- *Industry benchmarks:* Measure customer metrics such as adoptions, NPS, and CSAT against published industry metrics. It is also important to benchmark your GDRs, net dollar retention rates (NDRs), and customer long-term value (LTV) against other companies in your industry to determine where you stand.

- *Customer engagement:* Measure the level of customer engagement with your organization's industry-specific content, webinars, and events.

Real-World Examples

- *Salesforce:* Salesforce leverages industry research and benchmarking to provide its customers with comprehensive reports on market trends, customer behaviors, and best practices. This empowers its customer success teams to guide customers toward successful adoption and achieving desired outcomes.

- *HubSpot:* HubSpot conducts industry research to provide valuable insights to its customers, helping the company align its marketing and sales strategies with industry trends. This positions HubSpot as a trusted advisor and strengthens its customer relationships.

Why Industry Research and Benchmarking Aid Customer Retention

Leveraging industry research and benchmarking can significantly enhance upsell and cross-sell opportunities. Customer success teams utilize this data to provide customers with valuable insights and recommendations, establishing their organization as a trusted partner deeply committed to their success. This, in turn, bolsters the value proposition and nurtures long-term customer loyalty.

This approach enables customer success teams to proactively tackle customer challenges and anticipate their evolving needs by staying well-informed about industry trends. Such a proactive stance fosters trust and showcases a profound understanding of the customer's business.

Additionally, incorporating industry research and benchmarking empowers customer success teams to maintain a competitive advantage. They can offer customers unique and relevant insights that keep them ahead of competitors, solidifying the organization's position as an industry leader and fortifying customer relationships.

How Industry Research and Benchmarking Can Improve Upsell and Cross-Sell Opportunities

Industry research and benchmarking are practices that have the potential to significantly enhance upsell and cross-sell opportunities. The data obtained enables teams to pinpoint opportunities aligned with industry trends, customer behaviors, and market insights, ensuring their recommendations precisely match customer needs and contribute to revenue growth.

Leveraging the insights gathered, customer success teams can identify market gaps and propose product or service enhancements tailored to meet evolving customer demands. This proactive approach not only strengthens the potential for upselling and cross-selling but also presents customers with valuable solutions that address their changing needs.

The use of industry research and benchmarking allows customer success teams to craft personalized upsell and cross-sell recommendations that consider each customer's unique industry and business context. This personalized touch significantly increases the likelihood of success and enhances overall customer satisfaction.

Final Thoughts

Customer success teams must go beyond traditional customer support to drive customer satisfaction, retention, and revenue growth. Leveraging industry research and benchmarking empowers customer success teams to become trusted advisors, providing valuable insights and recommendations to customers.

By staying informed, benchmarking performance, and collaborating with industry experts, organizations can deliver exceptional value, improve customer retention, and unlock upsell and cross-sell opportunities.

Ultimately, incorporating industry research and benchmarking as a core strategy in customer success enhances the organization's competitive advantage, strengthens customer relationships, and positions the organization as an industry leader.

Part V: Data-Driven Customer Success

"Data beats emotions." — Sean Rad, co-founder of Tinder

Chapter Twenty-Four
Utilizing Customer Data Analytics and Insights for Successful Customer Success Strategies

Some of the most important tools for success as an enterprise company are customer data analytics and insights. By gathering and analyzing data from customer interactions and behaviors, companies can gain valuable insights that can help them improve their customer success strategies and ultimately increase customer retention and revenue.

In Part V of *Customer Success Mastery*, we'll examine the importance of gathering customer data and analyzing it to build an effective customer success strategy and drive intelligent decision-making.

How to Utilize Customer Data Analytics and Insights for Successful Customer Success Strategies

Customer data analytics is a powerful tool that allows businesses to gain a deeper understanding of their customers and drive success. Here's how your business can use customer data to provide analytics and insights that can drive customer retention and growth:

Data Capture

Capturing customer data is the first step in this process. Companies employ various methods to collect data from customer interactions and behaviors. One such method is transactional data, which provides insights into purchasing patterns, product preferences, and buying frequency. This data can be obtained through point-of-sale systems, e-commerce platforms, or loyalty programs.

Another method is analyzing customers' digital footprints, including website visits, social media interactions, and email engagement, using tools like web analytics, tracking pixels, and cookies. Businesses can also solicit feedback from customers directly through surveys, focus groups, or customer support interactions to gather qualitative data on customer sentiment, satisfaction, and pain points.

Extracting Insights

Once customer data is captured, businesses can utilize various analytical techniques to extract meaningful insights.

Segmentation and personalization are key strategies enabled by customer data analytics. Analyzing customer data allows businesses to segment their customer base according to demographic, behavioral, or psychographic characteristics. This segmentation allows for personalized marketing campaigns, product recommendations, and tailored customer experiences. When they understand the unique needs and preferences of different customer segments, companies can deliver targeted messaging and offerings that resonate with their audiences.

Methodology is another critical aspect of customer data analytics. It involves data cleaning, integration, and analysis using statistical techniques and algorithms. Data cleaning ensures accuracy and consistency, while data integration combines various data sources for a comprehensive view.

Predictive Models and Forecasting

Customer data analytics enables businesses to develop predictive models and forecasting techniques. By analyzing historical data, businesses can identify trends, patterns, and correlations that inform future decision-making. These insights allow companies to anticipate customer behavior, identify opportunities for cross-selling and upselling, and optimize pricing strategies.

Using Analytics and Insights to Improve Customer Success Strategies

Customer data analytics also plays a crucial role in improving customer success strategies. By analyzing customer data, businesses can identify pain points, bottlenecks, and areas for improvement in the customer journey. This data-driven approach empowers companies to develop strategies for enhancing the overall customer experience, resulting in increased customer satisfaction and retention.

Best Practices for Utilizing Customer Data Analytics and Insights for Customer Success

- *Data quality matters:* Ensure that the data collected is accurate, complete, and up to date. Inaccurate data can lead to flawed insights and ineffective strategies. Implement data validation and cleansing processes to maintain data quality.

- *Compliance and privacy:* Prioritize data privacy and compliance with relevant regulations such as GDPR or CCPA. Obtain explicit consent for data collection and processing and establish robust security measures to protect customer information.

- *Define clear objectives:* Start with well-defined goals for your customer data analytics initiatives. What specific insights are you looking to gain, and how will they contribute to customer success? Clear objectives help focus your efforts.

- *Customer segmentation:* Utilize data analytics to segment your customer base effectively. Understand the different characteristics and behaviors of customer segments to tailor your strategies, communications, and offerings accordingly.

- *Real-time data analysis:* Leverage real-time data analysis tools to stay updated on customer interactions and behaviors. Timely insights allow for agile decision-making and quick responses to customer needs and issues.

- *Predictive analytics:* Develop predictive models that anticipate customer behavior and preferences. This enables proactive engagement, such as personalized recommendations and targeted marketing efforts.

- *Cross-functional collaboration:* Foster collaboration between departments, including marketing, sales, customer support, and product development. Share insights and findings to ensure a unified approach to customer success.

- *Continuous learning:* Invest in ongoing training and development for your team to stay on top of the latest data analytics tools and techniques. Continuous learning ensures that your strategies remain effective and competitive.

- *Feedback loop:* Establish a feedback loop with customers. Encourage them to provide feedback through surveys, reviews, and direct interactions. This qualitative data complements quantitative analytics, providing a comprehensive view of customer sentiment.

- *Iterative improvement:* Use data-driven insights to continuously iterate and refine your customer success strategies. Regularly evaluate the effectiveness of your efforts and adjust as needed to meet changing customer expectations and market dynamics.

- *Data visualization:* Present insights in a visually compelling manner through data visualization tools. Clear and intuitive visuals help stakeholders across the organization understand and act upon insights.

- *Scalability:* Ensure that your data analytics infrastructure and processes are scalable to accommodate growth. As your customer base expands, your analytics capabilities should adapt to handle increased data volume and complexity.

- *Customer-centric approach:* Always prioritize the customer's perspective. Use analytics to identify pain points in the customer journey and take proactive steps to address them, improving overall customer satisfaction and retention.

- *Benchmarking:* Compare your performance and customer success metrics with industry benchmarks to gauge your competitiveness and identify areas where you can excel.

- *Ethical use of data:* Maintain ethical practices in data collection and analysis. Be transparent with customers about how their data is used and avoid exploiting personal information for unethical purposes.

Real-World Examples

- *Netflix:* Netflix is a company that has successfully utilized customer data analytics. The streaming giant gathers data on customer behavior, viewing preferences, and engagement with the platform to create personalized recommendations and improve the overall user experience. This has helped the company to retain customers and increase revenue.

- *Amazon:* Amazon uses customer data analytics to personalize product recommendations and improve the customer experience. It also uses data to optimize its supply chain and improve shipping times.

Why Customer Data Analytics and Insights Aid Customer Retention and Upsells

Customer data analytics and insights play a pivotal role in enhancing customer retention efforts within customer success teams. By harnessing the power of data, these teams gain a profound understanding of their customers' needs, preferences, and behaviors — an understanding that allows them to personalize their approach to each customer, providing tailored support and engagement that resonate on a personal level.

The ability to anticipate customer needs and proactively address concerns is a significant advantage offered by data analytics. By closely monitoring customer behavior and sentiment indicators, such as declining product usage or negative feedback, customer success teams can step in with timely assistance, preventing issues from escalating and potentially leading to customer churn.

Customer data analytics unveils opportunities for targeted upselling and cross-selling. Teams can identify which customers are most likely to benefit from additional products or services, tailoring their recommendations accordingly. This not only drives revenue growth but also demonstrates a deep understanding of the evolving needs of customers.

Data-driven communication strategies become possible, allowing teams to determine the most effective channels, timing, and content for engaging with customers. This precision enhances the likelihood of capturing the customer's attention and maintaining ongoing engagement.

Furthermore, data-backed insights help customer success teams pinpoint pain points in the customer journey, enabling them to implement solutions that genuinely enhance the customer experience. This focus on problem-solving and proactive support fosters trust and long-term loyalty. Customers appreciate vendors that actively contribute to their success, making them more inclined to continue their partnership.

Final Thoughts

The path to building lasting and mutually beneficial relationships with customers is paved with data. The use of customer data analytics and insights stands as a critical milestone on this path, empowering organizations to not only understand their customers but to proactively meet their needs and expectations, too.

In this exploration of the significance of customer data analytics, we have unearthed a treasure trove of strategies, best practices, and real-world examples that showcase the transformative potential of data-driven decision-making.

It's abundantly clear that capturing and harnessing customer data is not merely a technical endeavor but a strategic imperative. As organizations embark on this journey, they must prioritize data quality, compliance, and ethical practices while defining clear objectives and leveraging customer segmentation for personalized interactions. Real-time data analysis and predictive modeling emerge as dynamic tools for staying agile and proactive in the ever-evolving landscape of customer success.

However, the true power of customer data analytics lies not in the numbers alone but in the tangible impact it has on customer success. By identifying pain points, offering timely solutions, and personalizing engagements, organizations bolster customer satisfaction and retention. Data-driven insights also open doors to upsell and cross-sell opportunities, elevating revenue streams and customer lifetime value.

In the final analysis, the integration of data analytics into customer success strategies represents a transformative journey. It bridges the gap between assumptions and informed decisions and between generic interactions and personalized experiences. It empowers organizations to not only meet but anticipate customer needs, fostering a sense of partnership and trust.

As we navigate this data-driven landscape, the rewards are clear: improved customer retention, sustainable growth, and, most importantly, the satisfaction of knowing that our customer's success is our success.

Chapter Twenty-Five

Capturing and Reporting on Customer Success Metrics and KPIs

In the world of customer success, it's important to have a clear understanding of how your customers are using your product and how successful they are in achieving their desired outcomes. This is where customer success metrics and key performance indicators (KPIs) come into play.

In this chapter, we'll explore why capturing and reporting on customer success metrics is so important and the best practices to implement to ensure you get useful insights.

Why Capturing and Reporting on Customer Success Metrics and KPIs Matters

Capturing and reporting on customer success metrics and KPIs is critical for enterprise companies looking to optimize their customer success strategies. By measuring key metrics such as customer satisfaction, adoption, retention, and expansion, customer success teams can identify areas of improvement and track progress over time. With the right techniques and metrics in place, companies can strengthen their customer relationships, reduce churn, and increase revenue.

The process of capturing and reporting on customer success metrics and KPIs isn't just a recommended practice; it's an absolute necessity for enterprises aiming to fine-tune their customer success strategies. By meticulously measuring pivotal metrics such as customer satisfaction, adoption rates, retention rates, and expansion opportunities, customer success teams are empowered to pinpoint areas where improvements are required and, perhaps more importantly, gauge their progress over time. These metrics serve as a compass that guides companies toward strengthening their bonds with customers, curbing churn rates, and, ultimately, boosting their revenue streams.

In essence, these metrics act as a powerful diagnostic tool for companies, allowing them to identify pain points in their customer relationships, enabling swift intervention to rectify issues, and fostering proactive engagement with their customer base. For instance, tracking customer satisfaction can unveil areas where product or service enhancements are needed, while assessing adoption rates can provide insights into the effectiveness of onboarding and training programs. Furthermore, retention metrics clearly show customer loyalty, while expansion metrics illuminate opportunities for upselling and cross-selling additional services or products.

To underscore the significance of these metrics, let's imagine a software-as-a-service (SaaS) company that, after diligently monitoring its customer success metrics, discovers that a particular segment of its customer base exhibits low product adoption rates. Armed with this insight, the company can devise targeted strategies such as improved onboarding processes, educational resources, or personalized support to address this issue. As a result, customer satisfaction increases, churn decreases, and the potential for upselling premium features becomes more apparent.

Best Practices for Capturing and Reporting on Customer Success Metrics and KPIs

- *Set clear goals:* Identify what success looks like for your customers and establish clear, measurable goals for each stage of the customer journey.
- *Leverage technology:* Use customer success software or other tools to automate data collection and streamline reporting processes.
- *Collaborate cross-functionally:* Work with other departments, such as sales and product, to align on metrics and ensure everyone is working toward the same goals.

Real-World Examples

- *Salesforce:* The cloud-based software company uses a customer success platform to track and measure adoption, usage, and customer satisfaction. This has helped the company identify areas for improvement and optimize its customer success strategy.
- *Zendesk:* The customer service software company uses a combination of customer satisfaction (CSAT) scores, net promoter scores (NPS), and retention metrics to measure

customer success. By focusing on these metrics, they have been able to reduce churn and increase customer loyalty.

Why Capturing and Reporting on Customer Success Metrics and KPIs Aids Customer Retention

Capturing and reporting on customer success metrics and KPIs is a key strategy for retaining customers because it allows you to track and measure customer satisfaction, adoption, retention, and expansion.

By understanding how your customers are using your product and how successful they are in achieving their desired outcomes, you can identify areas that need improvement and proactively address issues before they become problems. This leads to happier, more engaged customers who are more likely to renew their subscriptions or contracts and recommend your product to others.

How Capturing and Reporting on Customer Success Metrics and KPIs Can Improve Upsell and Cross-Sell Opportunities

Capturing and reporting on customer success metrics and KPIs is more than just a routine exercise; it's a strategic imperative with the potential to unlock significant growth opportunities. These metrics guide customer success teams, helping them navigate the complex landscape of customer relationships. However, their impact doesn't stop at measuring past performance; when wielded effectively, they become powerful tools for driving upsell and cross-sell opportunities.

First and foremost, capturing and reporting on customer success metrics provides organizations with a comprehensive understanding of their customers' journey and satisfaction levels. It's like having a window into the hearts and minds of your customer base.

By analyzing data related to customer usage patterns, feedback, and overall satisfaction, customer success teams can identify opportunities to upsell additional products or services that align with customers' evolving needs. This deep insight enables teams to tailor their upsell strategies with precision, ensuring they offer solutions that genuinely resonate with the customer.

The ability to report on these metrics in a clear and compelling manner is also instrumental in building trust and credibility with customers. When customers see that an organization is actively monitoring their satisfaction and using data to improve their experience, the value of the existing partnership is reinforced and the door to cross-sell opportunities is opened. Customers are more likely to consider complementary offerings when they perceive a commitment to their success.

Final Thoughts

The world of customer success is undeniably enriched by the diligent practice of capturing and reporting on customer success metrics and KPIs. This chapter has shed light on the pivotal role these metrics play in enterprise companies' efforts to optimize their customer success strategies. The significance of these metrics cannot be overstated, as they serve as the guiding stars in the vast cosmos of customer relationships, leading businesses toward the twin goals of retention and growth.

By immersing themselves in the world of customer data, organizations can harness valuable insights into their customers' journeys and satisfaction levels. Armed with this knowledge, customer success teams are well-equipped to navigate the intricate terrain of customer relationships, identifying precise opportunities for upselling and cross-selling. The data-driven approach ensures that every recommendation aligns seamlessly with the customer's evolving needs, fostering an environment of trust and collaboration.

Moreover, the ability to present these insights clearly and persuasively is a cornerstone of success. Building credibility and trust with customers through transparent reporting opens doors to cross-sell opportunities, as customers appreciate a commitment to their success.

As we embrace the power of customer success metrics and KPIs, we enter an era where relationships are cultivated with precision, opportunities are seized proactively, and the customer journey is transformed into a delightful odyssey. These metrics not only hold the key to customer retention but also unlock the door to sustainable growth and a future where both organizations and their customers thrive in tandem.

Chapter Twenty-Six
Continuous Improvement and Innovation

Client success departments must embrace a culture of continuous improvement and innovation. This chapter explores how customer success teams can leverage these principles to enhance their performance, deliver exceptional customer experiences, and drive long-term success for enterprise companies.

What Do We Mean by Continuous Improvement and Innovation?

Continuous improvement, in the context of customer success, is an ongoing process aimed at enhancing the value and experience customer success teams give to customers. As a customer success manager (CSM), this means consistently seeking ways to better understand your customers' evolving needs, challenges, and goals. By actively engaging with customers, listening to their feedback, and analyzing data, you can identify areas where you can optimize your products, services, and support to exceed their expectations.

Why Do Continuous Improvement and Innovation Matter?

Continuous improvement is about being agile and responsive, adapting strategies and approaches based on customer feedback and market trends. By embracing this mindset, CSMs can build stronger and more meaningful relationships with customers, ensuring they consistently deliver exceptional value and help them achieve their desired outcomes. Ultimately, continuous improvement allows them to be proactive in addressing customer needs, enhance the customer's overall experience, and position themselves as trusted partners committed to the customer's success.

An example of a CSM using continuous improvement to help their customer could be in the context of a software company that provides a project management tool. The CSM regularly engages with their customers through regular check-ins and feedback sessions to understand their experience with the software.

During one of these check-ins, a customer expresses that they find it challenging to track progress on larger projects that involve multiple team members. The CSM takes note of this feedback and recognizes an opportunity for continuous improvement.

To address the customer's concern, the CSM collaborates with the product development team to propose enhancements to the software. They suggest implementing a new feature that allows users to create visual project timelines, assign tasks to specific team members, and track progress in real time. The CSM presents this idea to the customer and gathers their input to ensure it aligns with their needs.

After receiving approval from the customer, the CSM works closely with the development team to test and implement the new feature. Once it's ready, the CSM provides personalized training to the customer's team to ensure they fully understand and utilize the enhanced functionality.

The CSM continues to monitor the customer's usage of the new feature and gathers feedback on its effectiveness. They use this feedback to make any necessary adjustments and improvements, ensuring that the customer's experience with the software is continually optimized.

By actively seeking and implementing customer feedback, the CSM demonstrates a commitment to continuous improvement, resulting in a more tailored and valuable solution for the customer. This proactive approach not only addresses the customer's immediate needs but also strengthens the relationship, as the customer sees that their feedback is valued and acted upon. It also positions the CSM and the company as trusted partners invested in the customer's success.

Best Practices for Implementing Continuous Improvement and Innovation

- *Feedback loops:* Establish mechanisms for collecting feedback from customers, internal stakeholders, and team members. Regularly review and analyze this feedback to identify areas for improvement and innovation in the products or services you offer and ways to deliver a better customer experience.

- *Process optimization:* Continuously assess and refine internal processes to enhance efficiency, effectiveness, and scalability. Streamline workflows, automate repetitive tasks, and leverage technology solutions to optimize resource allocation and improve customer outcomes.

- *Innovation initiatives:* Encourage a culture of innovation by empowering team members to share ideas, experiment with new approaches, and contribute to problem-solving. Foster an environment that values creativity, risk-taking, and learning from failures.

Metrics to Measure

- *Net promoter score:* Assess whether customers are more likely to recommend your products or services after the improvements or innovations. An increase in NPS suggests that customers perceive added value.

- *Customer feedback volume:* Track the volume of customer feedback received, both positive and negative. An increase in feedback volume may indicate that customers are more engaged and vocal about their needs and concerns.

- *Time to implement improvements:* Measure the time it takes to implement suggested improvements or innovations. A decrease in this metric shows that your team is becoming more agile and responsive to customer feedback.

- *Feature adoption rate:* Monitor the adoption rate of new features or innovations among your customer base. Higher adoption rates suggest that customers are embracing the changes.

- *Feature usage:* Analyze how frequently and extensively customers are using new features or innovations. Increased usage indicates that these changes are valuable to customers.

Real-World Examples

- *Salesforce:* Salesforce's customer success team regularly collect feedback from customers through surveys, user groups, and customer advisory boards. They use this feedback to drive product enhancements and improve the overall customer experience, resulting in high customer satisfaction and retention rates.

- *Amazon Web Services (AWS):* AWS employs a culture of innovation and continuous improvement within its customer success department. The team encourages employees to come up with innovative solutions to address customer challenges and provides ongoing training and development opportunities to foster a culture of learning and growth.

Why Continuous Improvement and Innovation Aids Customer Retention

Continuous improvement and innovation are crucial for customer success teams to stay ahead of evolving customer needs and industry trends. By actively seeking feedback, optimizing processes, and embracing innovation, customer success departments can deliver exceptional customer experiences, proactively address customer pain points, and provide value-added solutions.

This approach builds trust, fosters long-term customer relationships, and increases customer loyalty, ultimately leading to higher customer retention rates.

How Continuous Improvement and Innovation Can Improve Upsell and Cross-Sell Opportunities

Continuous improvement and innovation are not just customer success buzzwords; they are dynamic strategies that can significantly enhance upsell and cross-sell opportunities. These twin principles serve as potent catalysts, propelling customer success teams toward deeper customer engagement and higher revenue streams.

Continuous improvement and innovation are grounded in the fundamental principle of understanding and fulfilling customer needs. By actively listening to customer feedback and monitoring their usage patterns, customer success teams gain unparalleled insights into evolving customer requirements. This invaluable knowledge allows teams to develop and refine products, services, and solutions that align precisely with customer expectations. When customers perceive that their needs are not only met but consistently exceeded, they become more receptive to upsell and cross-sell offers that can further enhance their experience.

Innovation, in particular, plays a pivotal role in uncovering new avenues for customer engagement. By exploring creative solutions and novel approaches, customer success teams can introduce additional value to customers, making upsell opportunities not only relevant but irresistible. For instance, a software provider may innovate by introducing cutting-edge features that offer enhanced functionality, presenting an ideal cross-sell opportunity for existing customers looking to expand their toolkit. Demonstrating a commitment to innovation can ignite a sense of curiosity and exploration among customers, driving them to explore new offerings.

Furthermore, continuous improvement and innovation empower customer success teams to develop a deep sense of trust and credibility with customers. When customers witness that their feedback is not only heard but actively integrated into product enhancements and service improvements, they gain confidence in the partnership. This trust becomes a bedrock for upsell and cross-sell opportunities. Customers are more likely to consider additional offerings from a provider they trust, knowing that the solutions will be tailored to their evolving needs.

Final Thoughts

By embracing feedback, optimizing processes, fostering innovation, and leveraging metrics, customer success departments can enhance customer satisfaction, drive retention, and unlock new revenue opportunities.

The journey of continuous improvement is an ongoing one, requiring adaptability, collaboration, and a commitment to delivering exceptional value to customers. By prioritizing continuous improvement and innovation, customer success teams can elevate their performance and contribute significantly to the overall success of the organization.

Chapter Twenty-Seven
Churn Analysis

It is important to recognize the impact that churn can have on a business's bottom line. Churn analysis is a vital part of a customer success strategy, as it allows businesses to identify and address the reasons why customers leave and take steps to prevent it from happening in the future.

In this chapter, we will explore what churn analysis is, how to do it, and real-world examples of where churn analysis is used as part of an effective customer success strategy.

What is Churn Analysis?

Customer churn analysis is the process of analyzing and understanding the factors that lead to customer churn. Churn is the rate at which customers discontinue their relationship with a company.

Churn analysis involves collecting and analyzing various data points, such as customer behavior, engagement patterns, product usage, customer feedback, and demographic information, to identify trends and patterns that correlate with churn. By utilizing advanced analytics tools and techniques, businesses can gain valuable insights into the reasons behind customer attrition and develop strategies to reduce churn rates.

Why Churn Analysis Matters

Customer churn analytics is used in several ways to support a company's customer retention efforts. Firstly, it helps identify high-risk customers by flagging warning signs or early indicators of potential churn. For example, if a customer suddenly reduces their use of a product or stops engaging with the company, they may be at risk of churning. Armed with this information, customer success teams can proactively reach out to these customers to offer personalized support and solutions to address their concerns and needs.

Secondly, churn analytics aids in the development of targeted retention strategies. By understanding the specific factors that contribute to churn, businesses can tailor their retention efforts and resources to address these pain points effectively. For instance, if the analysis consistently highlights a specific issue with a product feature, the company can prioritize fixing the problem to improve customer satisfaction and reduce churn.

Churn analysis can also inform product development and innovation. By analyzing patterns of churned customers and comparing them with the behavior of retained customers, companies can gain valuable insights into what features or improvements are most valued by their customer base. This information can guide future product enhancements that keep the company competitive and meet the evolving needs of its customers.

Best Practices for Executing Churn Analysis

- *Gather data from multiple sources:* It's important to gather and analyze customer data from several sources, such as customer feedback, customer support interactions, and product usage data.
- *Create a customer health score:* Create a customer health score that combines different metrics to identify customers who are at risk of churning. (More on customer health scores in Chapter 8.)
- *Monitor customer engagement:* Tracking customer engagement reveals how actively customers are using a product or service and identifies patterns that suggest potential churn.
- *Segmentation:* Segment customers by usage, demographics, or other criteria to identify groups that are more likely to churn.

Real-World Examples

- *Netflix:* Netflix analyzes millions of data points to determine what content customers are watching, skipping, and rating highly. This information helps the company make more informed decisions about what content to produce and what content to remove, ultimately leading to higher customer satisfaction and retention rates.
- *HubSpot:* HubSpot developed a customer health score that takes into account various metrics such as product usage, customer feedback, and support interactions. This score helps

the customer success team identify at-risk customers and take action to prevent churn.

Why Churn Analysis Aids Customer Retention

When customer success teams understand why customers churn, they can take steps to improve current customers' experiences with the company and keep them happy. Ultimately, knowing why customers churn can prevent others from churning for the same or similar reasons.

Conducting churn analysis also allows businesses to gain a better understanding of their customers and their needs, ultimately leading to higher levels of customer satisfaction and loyalty.

Final Thoughts

Churn analysis is a critical component of any customer success strategy. It's the process of examining customer behavior and identifying why customers leave a business.

When they understand why customers leave, businesses can take steps to prevent it from happening in the future, improving customer retention and, ultimately, increasing revenue. Techniques such as creating a customer health score, tracking customer engagement, and segmenting customers enable businesses to gain valuable insights into their customers and their needs. Meanwhile, measuring key metrics such as churn rate, customer retention rate, and lifetime value (LTV) reveals the effectiveness of efforts to prevent churn.

Chapter Twenty-Eight
Root Cause Analysis

Just addressing the issues that arise with customers isn't enough; an effective customer success team should also identify the root causes of those issues. Root cause analysis (RCA) is a valuable tool for identifying the underlying reasons for customer complaints or issues and addressing them effectively to improve customer satisfaction and retention.

In this chapter, we will explore how customer success teams can use RCA to enhance the customer success strategy.

What is Root Cause Analysis?

Root cause analysis is a systematic approach used to identify the underlying causes of an issue or problem. By determining the root cause, a customer success team can address the underlying issue and prevent the problem from recurring in the future.

RCA is an indispensable tool within any customer success team's toolkit. It forms the foundation of their problem-solving approach, enabling them to go beyond surface-level issues and delve deep into the underlying causes of problems or challenges customers may encounter.

The approach involves thorough investigation, data analysis, and a commitment to understanding not just what happened but why it happened. By adopting this approach, customer success teams can ensure solutions are not just quick fixes but designed to eliminate the source of the problem.

Why Root Cause Analysis Matters

The value of RCA cannot be overstated. When you identify and address root causes, you don't just resolve the immediate issue; instead, you create a proactive strategy to prevent similar problems from arising in the future. This is pivotal in enhancing overall customer satisfaction and retention rates. It reflects your dedication to providing sustainable solutions that foster long-term success for your customers.

By employing RCA, customer success teams not only demonstrate their commitment to resolving issues but also their dedication to continuous improvement. Customer success professionals can refine processes, work to enhance products and services, and adapt strategies based on the insights gained. This not only benefits individual customers but also contributes to the evolution and growth of the organization as a whole.

Best Practices for Implementing Root Cause Analysis

Incorporating root cause analysis into your problem-solving toolkit is a strategic imperative for any customer success team. Here, we outline best practices for implementing root cause analysis:

- *Engage in collaborative brainstorming sessions:* Collaborative brainstorming sessions serve as a forum for open dialogue where customers can articulate any problems or challenges they might be experiencing with your product or service. By actively involving customers in problem identification, you gain valuable firsthand insights into their pain points and foster a sense of partnership in addressing these issues.

- *Conduct comprehensive interviews:* Beyond group brainstorming, conduct one-on-one interviews with customers and key stakeholders. These interviews provide an opportunity to delve deeper into specific issues, allowing customers to express their concerns in a more personalized manner. Through thoughtful questioning and active listening, you can extract nuanced details that might not surface in larger group settings.

- *Analyze data and feedback:* Gather and analyze the data and feedback obtained from customer interactions. This data could encompass a wide range of inputs, from quantitative metrics to qualitative anecdotes. A meticulous examination of this information is crucial to discern patterns, trends, and potential root causes of the issues identified.

- *Leverage fishbone diagrams for clarity:* Employ a fishbone diagram, also known as an Ishikawa or cause-and-effect diagram, to visually map out potential causes of the problems you have identified. This structured approach allows you to categorize factors that could contribute to the issues, such as people, processes, equipment, or external influences. By organizing these potential causes systematically, you gain clarity and insight into the complex web of factors at play.

Metrics to Measure

- *Problem resolution rate:* This metric measures how effectively RCA is leading to problem resolution. It is the percentage of identified issues that have been successfully resolved at their root rather than merely addressing symptoms or applying quick fixes. A high problem-resolution rate indicates that RCA is contributing to long-term solutions and customer satisfaction.

- *Repeat incidents or issues:* Track the number of repeat incidents or issues related to the same root cause. If the same problem recurs frequently, it suggests that the root cause has not been adequately addressed. A decreasing trend in repeat incidents demonstrates that RCA is effective in preventing the reoccurrence of issues, thereby reducing customer frustration and support costs.

- *Customer satisfaction improvement:* Measure changes in customer satisfaction scores, such as CSAT or NPS, before and after implementing RCA-driven solutions. An increase in customer satisfaction indicates that RCA is positively impacting the customer experience by resolving issues, enhancing product quality, and reducing downtime.

These three metrics provide a holistic view of how RCA is contributing to problem-solving, issue prevention, and customer satisfaction. By monitoring these key indicators, you can assess the overall effectiveness of your RCA process and make necessary adjustments to continually improve its impact.

Real-World Examples

Starbucks

The global coffeehouse chain Starbucks employs root cause analysis to continuously improve customer experiences at its stores.

Suppose Starbucks receives consistent feedback from customers about long wait times at certain locations. In that case, they would initiate an RCA process to determine the root cause of these delays. This could involve observing store operations, interviewing baristas and customers, and analyzing data on order processing times.

By identifying root causes, such as understaffing during peak hours or inefficient layout designs, Starbucks can implement changes like optimizing staffing schedules or store layouts. These improvements lead to shorter wait times, increased customer satisfaction, and potentially higher sales through improved customer experiences.

Marriott International

The hospitality giant Marriott International employs root cause analysis within its customer success strategy.

Let's imagine that Marriott receives feedback from guests about recurring issues, such as room cleanliness or reservation mix-ups. The company utilizes RCA techniques to investigate these problems thoroughly. This might include gathering feedback from guests, conducting internal audits, and analyzing reservation and check-in processes.

Once the root causes are identified, Marriott can implement corrective actions like enhanced staff training or improvements in their reservation system. By addressing these fundamental issues, Marriott ensures smoother guest experiences, fewer complaints, and increased customer loyalty, ultimately driving long-term success.

Why Root Cause Analysis Aids Customer Retention

By addressing the root cause of an issue, customer success teams can prevent the problem from recurring in the future, improving customer satisfaction and retention. This approach demonstrates to the customer that their concerns are being taken seriously and addressed in a proactive manner, which can lead to increased loyalty and advocacy.

How This Strategy Can Improve Upsell and Cross-Sell Opportunities

When customer success teams address the root cause of an issue, they also have the opportunity to identify potential areas for improvement or where the customer could benefit from a new or upgraded product. By taking a proactive approach to identifying and addressing customer needs, customer success teams can improve their overall relationship with the customer and identify opportunities to expand their business with them.

Final Thoughts

Root cause analysis is a valuable tool for customer success teams to identify and address the underlying causes of issues or complaints from customers. By taking a proactive approach to problem-solving, customer success teams can improve customer satisfaction and retention rates and identify opportunities for upselling and cross-selling.

By implementing RCA techniques and measuring the success of their efforts, customer success teams can continuously improve their processes and better serve their customers.

Chapter Twenty-Nine
Data-Driven Decision-Making in Customer Success

As we've explored in depth throughout Part V, data-driven customer success is intrinsically tied to the dynamic realm of customer data analytics and insights. This powerful approach harnesses the wealth of information generated by customer interactions and behaviors, propelling customer success strategies to new heights. Data-driven decision-making represents the culmination of a well-structured process that involves meticulous data collection, rigorous analysis, and insightful reporting.

In the context of data-driven decision-making, the journey commences with the systematic collection of customer data from various touchpoints and sources. This treasure trove of information includes customer feedback, usage patterns, engagement metrics, and more. Through the lens of advanced analytics, this raw data undergoes a transformative journey, evolving into meaningful insights that unveil hidden patterns, emerging trends, and areas requiring improvement that might have otherwise remained elusive. This analytical phase isn't static; it's an ongoing process that adapts and evolves as customer behaviors and market dynamics change.

Data-driven decision-making is not a solitary endeavor; it thrives within an environment of continuous improvement and innovation. This dynamic approach compels customer success teams to be agile and adaptable, constantly seeking ways to better understand their customers' ever-evolving needs, challenges, and aspirations. By actively engaging with customers, listening attentively to their feedback, and analyzing data with precision, customer success professionals embark on a constant journey of enhancement. The insights derived from data empower customer success teams to optimize products, services, and support offerings, consistently striving to exceed customer expectations.

Ultimately, data-driven decision-making is the driving force behind customer success strategies that deliver not only results but also remarkable customer experiences. It is the embodiment of the modern approach to customer-centricity, where data serves as a compass guiding customer success teams toward their ultimate destination: unwavering customer satisfaction, reduced churn, and increased revenue. In this ever-evolving landscape, the ability to harness the power of data and transform it into actionable insights is a game-changer, enabling customer success professionals to not only meet but exceed customer expectations while propelling their enterprise to new heights of growth and prosperity.

Why Data-Driven Decision-Making Matters

Among the many transformative approaches that have emerged, data-driven decision-making has risen to prominence as the new strategic imperative. At the heart of data-driven decision-making in customer success lies the recognition that data is a veritable goldmine of insights. Every customer interaction, product usage pattern, and support request generates valuable information. By harnessing this data, customer success teams can unravel profound insights into customer behavior, preferences, and needs. This data-driven approach empowers organizations to make informed, strategic decisions that significantly impact customer satisfaction and loyalty.

Data-driven decision-making serves as the bedrock for personalization and customized experiences. By analyzing customer data, organizations can tailor their interactions, communications, and solutions to meet the unique needs of each customer. This level of personalization fosters deeper customer relationships, as customers feel understood and valued. It goes beyond surface-level personalization and extends to anticipating customer needs and preferences, creating truly meaningful and lasting connections.

Predictive analytics, a cornerstone of data-driven decision-making, enables customer success teams to anticipate future trends and customer behavior. By analyzing historical data, organizations can develop predictive models that forecast customer churn, identify upsell opportunities, and even predict support ticket volumes. Armed with this foresight, customer success teams can take proactive measures to mitigate risks, seize opportunities, and stay ahead of the curve.

Data-driven decision-making also enhances operational efficiency and leads to cost savings. Customer success teams can free up valuable time and resources by automating data collection and analysis processes. This efficiency translates into more effective resource allocation, freeing up time for focusing on high-impact initiatives that drive customer success.

Best Practices for Data-Driven Decision-Making

- Establish robust systems to collect and analyze customer data, including demographics, usage patterns, feedback, and interactions.

- Leverage tools like customer relationship management (CRM) software and analytics platforms to consolidate and analyze this data effectively.

- Utilize data to segment customers based on their characteristics, preferences, and engagement levels. Segmentation enables customer success teams to personalize their interactions, communication, and support, providing tailored experiences that resonate with each customer segment.

- Implement predictive analytics models to forecast customer behavior, identify potential churn risks, and proactively address customer needs. By leveraging historical data, machine learning algorithms can help predict customer satisfaction, engagement, and propensity to purchase additional products or services.

- Map out the entire customer journey, identifying key touchpoints, pain points, and opportunities for improvement. Use data to understand customer behavior at each stage and make data-driven adjustments to enhance the overall experience.

Metrics to Measure

- *Customer satisfaction score:* Measure CSAT through surveys and feedback mechanisms to gauge how well your customer success efforts are meeting their needs and expectations.

- *Net promoter score:* Assess customer loyalty and their likelihood of recommending your products or services to others. NPS provides valuable insights into customer advocacy and helps identify potential brand evangelists.

- *Customer retention rate (CRR):* Measure the percentage of customers who continue to use your products or services over a specified period. A high CRR indicates effective customer success efforts and customer satisfaction.

- *Upsell and cross-sell revenue:* Track the revenue generated from upselling and cross-selling activities to measure the effectiveness of data-driven decision-making in driving additional sales within the existing customer base.

Real-World Examples

- *Amazon:* Amazon leverages its vast customer data to personalize product recommendations, offer personalized marketing campaigns, and enhance the overall customer experience. By analyzing customer behavior and purchase history, Amazon delivers highly relevant and targeted suggestions, driving increased sales and customer loyalty.

- *Netflix:* Netflix utilizes data-driven decision-making to recommend personalized content based on viewers' preferences and viewing history. Recommendation algorithms analyze user behavior and ratings to provide a curated content selection, leading to increased customer engagement and retention.

Why Data-Driven Decision-Making Aids Customer Retention

Data-driven decision-making in customer success offers a profound understanding of customer needs and allows teams to delve into their customers' preferences, pain points, and expectations by dissecting valuable data. Armed with these insights, organizations can craft tailored solutions and deliver exceptional experiences that resonate deeply with their customers.

Data-driven strategies are instrumental in proactive issue resolution. By leveraging data analytics, customer success teams can swiftly identify potential problems on the horizon and take proactive measures to mitigate them. This approach not only minimizes customer dissatisfaction but also serves as a robust churn prevention mechanism, ensuring that customers remain content and loyal.

Data-driven decision-making also serves as the bedrock for driving personalization initiatives. The insights gleaned from customer data form the foundation upon which personalized interactions are built. When customers perceive a brand's efforts to understand and value their individual preferences, it fosters a deeper sense of engagement and loyalty.

In essence, data-driven personalization transforms satisfied customers into devoted advocates who not only stay loyal but also actively champion the brand, amplifying its reach and influence in the market.

How This Strategy Can Improve Upsell and Cross-Sell Opportunities

Data analytics and data-driven decision-making unveil a world of potential, guiding customer success teams toward lucrative upsell and cross-sell opportunities.

By meticulously analyzing customer data encompassing behavior, preferences, and purchase history, organizations uncover the breadcrumbs leading to upsell and cross-sell prospects. Armed with these insights, customer success teams can craft precise and targeted offerings that seamlessly align with each customer's unique needs and interests.

But data-driven decision-making doesn't stop at merely identifying opportunities — it extends to predicting customer propensity. Through the formidable capabilities of predictive analytics, organizations gain the power to anticipate customer behavior and pinpoint those most amenable to upsell and cross-sell offers. This strategic foresight is invaluable as it allows for the personalized approach of targeting these receptive customers with tailor-made recommendations. Consequently, the likelihood of successful upsells and cross-sells soars, bolstering both customer satisfaction and the organization's bottom line.

In this data-driven landscape, communication and offers are not generic; they are meticulously tailored for maximum impact. The insights derived from data analytics empower customer success teams to personalize every facet of their interactions. From communication styles to the very essence of the offers presented, each element is meticulously crafted to resonate with individual customers. This level of personalization ensures that recommendations and incentives are not only relevant but also irresistibly compelling.

Final Thoughts

In the expansive landscape of "Part V: Data-Driven Customer Success," the significance of data-driven decision-making for customer success has become increasingly evident. This strategic approach serves as a linchpin for enterprise companies striving to optimize their customer success strategies. By immersing themselves in the sea of customer data, these organizations unlock a treasure trove of insights into intricate details like customer behavior, preferences, and evolving needs. This newfound understanding empowers them to navigate the customer journey with unparalleled precision, ultimately leading to customized approaches that boost customer retention and unlock tantalizing upsell and cross-sell opportunities.

The real-world successes of industry giants like Amazon and Netflix paint a vivid picture of the transformative power of data-driven decision-making. These companies have mastered the art of delivering hyper-personalized experiences, resulting in strengthened customer loyalty and substantial revenue growth. Through the systematic application of data collection and analysis, customer segmentation, predictive analytics, and the intricacies of customer journey mapping, these trailblazers harness data to guide their strategic choices. They embody the notion that data-driven decision-making is not just an option but a necessity, propelling them ahead in a fiercely competitive landscape while nurturing enduring customer relationships.

As Part V has unveiled the secrets of data-driven customer success, it has become clear that embracing this approach is the key to unlocking the future of enterprise success. With data as their guiding star, organizations can navigate the complex maze of customer experiences, adapt with agility, and craft strategies that resonate deeply with their diverse range of customers.

In this era of customer-centricity, the ability to transform data into actionable insights isn't merely a competitive edge; it's the cornerstone upon which remarkable customer success outcomes are built.

Part VI: Customer Support and Technology

"While a technology company might have the best product in the world, great customer support is the glue that makes customers stick around." — David Cancel, CEO of Drift

Types of Customer Support Channels and How to Implement Them for Exceptional Customer Experience

Customer support is an integral component of the broader field of customer success, playing a pivotal role in shaping a customer's overall experience with a company. A customer's perception of a business often hinges on effective communication channels between them and a customer support team.

In this chapter, we delve into the multifaceted world of customer support, examining the various types of support channels available and providing insights into how to implement them strategically to deliver an exceptional customer experience.

Why Having a Well-Structured Customer Support System Matters

The importance of a well-structured customer support ecosystem cannot be overstated. It serves as the frontline of interaction between a company and its customers, serving as a lifeline for addressing inquiries, resolving issues, and providing assistance.

The diversity of customer support channels available today is vast, ranging from traditional channels such as phone and email to more contemporary options like live chat, social media, and self-service portals. Each channel has its unique advantages, and the key lies in understanding the customer's preferences and needs to provide an optimal experience.

Implementing these support channels strategically involves several critical considerations. Firstly, it necessitates a deep understanding of your customer base. Knowing your customers' demographics, preferences, and pain points helps in tailoring the choice and deployment of support channels. For instance, tech-savvy customers might prefer self-service options like FAQs and online knowledge bases, while others may seek personalized assistance on the phone or through live chat.

Secondly, the integration of these channels into a seamless and coherent omnichannel experience is paramount. Customers expect a consistent level of service regardless of the channel they use, and this requires robust systems and well-trained support agents capable of providing a unified experience. Ensuring that customer data is accessible across channels to avoid repetition and maintain context is crucial in this regard.

Constant monitoring and feedback collection are essential to continuously improve your support channels. Regularly gauging customer satisfaction, response times, and issue resolution rates can help identify areas in need of refinement or expansion. This iterative approach is fundamental in staying agile and responsive to evolving customer needs and expectations.

Different Customer Support Channels

- *Email support:* Email is one of the most common customer support channels. It is easy to use and can be used for both simple and complex queries. Expect to get the best results when you ensure responses are sent promptly and communication is personalized.

- *Phone support:* Phone support is another popular channel that provides customers with instant access to support representatives. This channel is best for customers who need quick answers to their queries. However, it can be costly and time-consuming to implement.

- *Live chat support:* Live chat is a real-time communication channel that allows customers to chat with support representatives. It's a popular channel for e-commerce businesses as it provides customers with quick access to support. Ensuring that representatives are available to respond promptly is crucial.

- *Social media support:* Social media is becoming an increasingly popular channel for customer support. It allows customers to connect with companies through various social media platforms. Your organization will need a dedicated team to monitor and respond to queries on social media.

Metrics to Measure

- *Response time:* The time it takes for a support representative to respond to a customer's query is an important metric to measure. Customers expect prompt responses, and slow response times can result in frustration.

- *First contact resolution rate:* This metric is the percentage of customer queries that are resolved on the first contact. High first contact resolution rates indicate that support representatives are knowledgeable and efficient.

- *Customer satisfaction (CSAT) score:* CSAT measures how satisfied customers are with their support experience. It is important to measure CSAT regularly to identify areas that need improvement.

Real-World Examples

- *Amazon:* Amazon has a comprehensive customer support system that includes email, phone, and live chat support. The e-commerce giant's support representatives are available 24/7 to provide customers with quick and efficient guidance.

- *Zappos:* Zappos is known for its exceptional customer service. The company provides support through phone, email, and live chat. Zappos also has a dedicated team to respond to queries on social media platforms.

Why Customer Support Channels Aid Customer Retention

Effective customer support channels significantly contribute to customer retention because they play a crucial role in shaping the overall customer experience. These channels serve as a lifeline for customers, offering quick and accessible solutions to their inquiries and concerns.

When customers encounter issues or have questions, available and responsive support channels not only address their immediate needs but also demonstrate the company's commitment to their satisfaction. This level of attention and assistance fosters trust and loyalty.

In addition, customer support channels provide opportunities for companies to gather valuable feedback directly from customers. By actively listening to customer concerns, businesses can identify pain points, areas for improvement, and emerging trends in customer needs. This feedback loop allows companies to adapt their products, services, and strategies to align more closely with customer expectations, leading to higher satisfaction and retention rates.

Final Thoughts

Customer support plays an indispensable role in the customer success journey. As we've explored in this chapter, it serves as the critical link between a company and its customers, and the effectiveness of support channels is of paramount importance for shaping the overall customer experience. It is not an exaggeration to say that the success of a business often hinges on the strength of its customer support system.

Having a well-structured customer support ecosystem is essential for addressing customer inquiries, resolving issues, and providing assistance promptly and effectively. The diversity of support channels available today, ranging from traditional to contemporary options, provides an opportunity to tailor the support experience to individual customer preferences and needs.

Strategic implementation of these support channels is a multifaceted endeavor that requires a deep understanding of the customer base, seamless integration for an omnichannel experience, and a continuous improvement mindset fueled by monitoring and feedback collection. Companies that excel in these areas stand poised to deliver exceptional customer experiences, foster trust and loyalty, and ensure long-term customer retention.

Lastly, metrics such as response time, first contact resolution rate, and CSAT score provide invaluable insights into the effectiveness of support efforts, guiding organizations toward areas of improvement and innovation. Real-world examples like Amazon and Zappos demonstrate the power of comprehensive customer support systems in ensuring customer satisfaction and loyalty.

Ultimately, the role of customer support channels in aiding customer retention cannot be overstated. By offering timely and accessible solutions, fostering trust through responsive assistance, and actively listening to customer feedback, businesses can not only retain their valued customers but also position themselves as customer-centric industry leaders, propelling their success in the competitive landscape of today's business world.

Chapter Thirty-One
Self-Service Portals

As customer expectations continue to expand, enterprises need to find ways to meet them while still managing costs. One solution that has gained popularity in recent years is the self-service portal. A self-service portal allows customers to access information, support, and other resources on their own schedule without the need for direct interaction with a support agent.

In this chapter, we will explore how self-service portals can make customer success teams more efficient, improve customer satisfaction, and generate increased revenue.

What Are Self-Service Portals?

Self-service support portals are digital platforms designed to empower customers to find solutions and resolve issues on their own without needing direct assistance from customer support agents. They are becoming increasingly popular among enterprises as they offer a way to meet customer expectations while reducing support costs.

These portals typically offer a comprehensive knowledge base that includes FAQs, troubleshooting guides, video tutorials, product documentation, and other resources. The goal is to provide customers with quick and easy access to information and assistance, enhancing their overall experience and reducing the need for traditional support channels.

Why Self-Service Portals Matter

Self-service portals benefit both customers and businesses in various ways.

For customers, these portals offer convenience and flexibility, as they can access information at any time, from anywhere, without waiting for support agents to become available. Customers can troubleshoot problems independently, which empowers them with a sense of control and ownership over their experiences with the product or service. Customers can also learn at their own pace, accessing relevant resources whenever they encounter challenges or wish to explore new features.

From a business perspective, self-service portals can significantly reduce a customer support team's workload, as many routine and repetitive inquiries can be handled through the portal. This efficiency allows support agents to focus on more complex and critical customer issues, improving overall response times and service quality.

Self-service portals can contribute to cost savings, as fewer support resources are needed to manage customer inquiries. Additionally, by analyzing user behavior and interactions on the portal, businesses can gain insights into customer needs, pain points, and preferences, enabling them to continuously improve the portal's content and user experience.

Best Practices for Implementing Effective Self-Service Portals

To be effective, self-service support portals must be user-friendly, well-organized, and regularly updated with relevant and accurate information. They should have intuitive search functionalities and clear navigation, enabling customers to find the answers they seek quickly. Regularly monitoring and analyzing portal usage and customer feedback can help identify areas for improvement and ensure that the portal meets customers' evolving needs.

Here are some best practices to follow when implementing a self-service portal:

- *Design the portal with user experience in mind:* The portal should be designed with the user in mind, providing easy-to-use navigation, intuitive search functionality, and clear, concise content.

- *Provide a robust knowledge base:* The portal should include an extensive knowledge base that covers frequently asked questions, troubleshooting steps, and other helpful resources.

- *Offer multichannel support:* The portal should provide customers with multiple ways to access support, such as chatbots, email, and phone support.

- *Employ automation:* Automation can be used to streamline processes and reduce manual work. For example, chatbots can be used to handle simple queries, freeing up agents to focus on more complex issues.

Metrics to Measure

- *Usage metrics:* The number of users accessing the portal, the frequency of usage, and the types of content accessed can provide insights into customer needs and preferences.
- *Customer satisfaction metrics:* Surveys or feedback forms can be used to gauge customer satisfaction with the self-service portal experience.
- *Cost savings metrics:* Enterprises should track the cost savings associated with the implementation of a self-service portal, including reductions in support tickets and agent time.

Real-World Examples

- *Salesforce:* Salesforce's Trailhead is a self-service portal that provides customers with access to resources, training, and support for Salesforce products. Customers can use the portal to complete courses and earn badges, improving their skills and knowledge of Salesforce products. The portal has been a major success, with over 20 million users worldwide.
- *HubSpot:* HubSpot's Knowledge Base provides customers with access to a wealth of resources, including articles, videos, and support documentation. The portal is designed with the user in mind, making it easy to navigate and find relevant information. As a result, HubSpot has seen a significant reduction in support tickets and improved customer satisfaction.

Why Self-Service Portals Aid Customer Retention

Self-service portals help organizations retain customers because they provide the information and support they need on their own schedule in a navigable and accessible format.

By providing customers with easy access to resources, enterprises can reduce the need for direct support interactions, freeing up support agents to focus on more complex issues that will aid customer retention in the long term. Additionally, self-service portals can improve customer satisfaction by providing customers with a consistent and reliable support experience. Happy customers are more likely to stick with the business and not look for alternative solutions.

How Self-Service Portals Can Improve Upsell and Cross-Sell Opportunities

By providing customers with a positive support experience through self-service portals, enterprises can improve their chances of upselling and cross-selling. Customers who have a positive experience are more likely to view the enterprise positively and be receptive to additional product offerings.

By providing relevant product information, tutorials, and demos, customers can be educated and informed about the full range of products and services available, which can lead to increased sales.

Final Thoughts

A self-service portal is a valuable tool for customer success teams as it provides customers with a convenient and accessible way to find answers to their questions and troubleshoot issues.

When customers can support themselves, customer success teams can focus on higher-value activities, such as proactive outreach and strategic planning. Moreover, self-service portals can help reduce customer churn, as they provide customers with a sense of control and autonomy over their experience with a product or service. By providing valuable content and resources, companies can educate customers on the value of additional offerings and encourage them to invest in these products or services.

Chapter Thirty-Two

Chatbots and AI-Powered Customer Service

As customer expectations continue to evolve, businesses must seek ways to provide fast, efficient, and personalized support to their customers. Some of the emerging technologies that have proved useful in achieving these objectives are chatbots and customer service powered by artificial intelligence (AI).

In this chapter, we will discuss how enterprises can use these technologies to improve customer success.

Why Chatbots and AI-Powered Customer Service Matter

Chatbots and AI-powered customer service have revolutionized customer support, and businesses can leverage these technologies to deliver excellent customer success. These tools provide customers with instant and personalized support, reducing wait times, improving customer satisfaction, and increasing engagement.

Artificial intelligence can significantly increase efficiency and reduce the need for extensive staff in customer support teams. One way AI achieves this is through the implementation of AI-powered chatbots and virtual assistants. These intelligent systems can handle a wide range of customer inquiries and routine tasks, such as answering FAQs, providing product information, and guiding customers through troubleshooting processes. By automating these interactions,

AI-powered chatbots can handle a large volume of customer queries simultaneously, significantly reducing the workload of human agents.

AI can also assist in automating repetitive tasks within customer support operations. For example, AI can categorize and prioritize customer tickets, assign them to the appropriate agents based on their expertise, and even draft standardized responses for common issues. This automation streamlines the support process, allowing human agents to focus on more complex and specialized tasks that require human empathy, problem-solving, and critical thinking skills.

AI-driven analytics and data processing also play a crucial role in improving efficiency. By analyzing customer data, AI can identify trends, patterns, and customer preferences, enabling organizations to personalize their support and proactively address customer needs. This data-driven approach optimizes the support workflow and enhances customer experiences, leading to increased customer satisfaction and loyalty.

Best Practices for Implementing Chatbots and AI-Powered Customer Service

- *Define your goals:* Businesses should identify the problems they intend to solve with chatbots and AI-powered customer service. This will help them create a tailored experience for their customers.
- *Choose the right platform:* There are many chatbot and AI-powered customer service platforms available, and businesses should select one that aligns with their goals and objectives.

- *Personalize the chatbots:* Personalizing chatbots helps customers feel valued and understood. Enterprises should create chatbots that mimic human conversation and understand customers' needs.

- *Train the chatbots:* Chatbots should be trained to handle various situations and answer customer queries effectively. This will ensure that customers receive relevant and accurate responses.

Metrics to Measure

- *Customer satisfaction rate:* This metric is the percentage of customers that are satisfied with the chatbot and AI-powered customer service experience.

- *Response time:* This metric is the time taken for the chatbot to respond to a customer query.

- *First contact resolution rate:* This is the percentage of customer queries resolved on the first contact.

Real-World Examples

- *Bank of America:* The Bank of America's chatbot, Erica, helps customers with account management, bill payments, and money transfers.

- *Sephora:* Sephora launched its chatbot on Kik Messenger, allowing customers to get personalized product recommendations and makeup tutorials.

Why This Strategy Works in Retaining Customers

Chatbots and AI-powered customer service help retain customers because they offer instant, personalized, and efficient support. Customers appreciate getting quick and efficient resolutions to their queries and are more likely to return to a business that offers this kind of support.

Final Thoughts

By reducing the need for manual intervention and streamlining processes, AI and chatbots enable customer support teams to operate more efficiently with fewer staff members. This not only results in cost savings but also enables businesses to scale their support operations more effectively without increasing staffing requirements linearly.

However, it's important to note that while AI can enhance efficiency and reduce staff needs, it is not meant to replace human agents entirely. Human touch and empathy remain essential in certain situations, particularly when dealing with complex and emotionally sensitive customer interactions. Hence, a harmonious integration of AI and human support can create a synergy that maximizes efficiency, cost-effectiveness, and overall customer satisfaction in customer support organizations.

Chapter Thirty-Three

Customer Success Management Software

In today's fast-paced and highly competitive business world, companies need to invest in technologies that help them stay ahead of the curve. One such technology has gained significant popularity in recent years: customer success management (CSM) software. This powerful tool can help your customer success team improve customer satisfaction, reduce churn, and increase revenue.

In this chapter, we will discuss how customer success teams can leverage CSM software to streamline their operations, increase customer retention rates, and drive business growth. We will explore the best practices for implementing the software, the metrics you'll need to measure success, and real-world examples of how companies have successfully implemented CSM software. We will also discuss how this strategy can improve upsell and cross-sell opportunities and provide a chart to help visualize the benefits.

Why Customer Success Management Software Matters

Customer success management software has emerged as a potent force that more and more companies are harnessing to maintain a competitive edge. This innovative technology is not merely an option but a strategic necessity for modern businesses looking to thrive. By adopting CSM software, organizations empower their customer success teams with a dynamic and comprehensive toolkit designed to enhance every facet of customer engagement.

Customer success is no longer a reactive endeavor — it has evolved into a proactive and strategic discipline, and CSM software is at the forefront of this transformation. This software offers a robust suite of features that streamline customer interactions, bolstering the efficiency and effectiveness of customer success teams. It enables teams to gain in-depth insights into customer behavior, preferences, and pain points, facilitating a deeper understanding of each customer's unique journey.

Moreover, CSM software facilitates the development and execution of personalized strategies, tailoring interactions and solutions to meet the specific needs of individual customers. This personalization fosters stronger relationships, as customers feel understood and valued, resulting in heightened satisfaction levels. By proactively addressing potential issues and offering proactive solutions, organizations can significantly reduce churn rates, ensuring that customers remain loyal over the long term.

CSM software also plays a pivotal role in driving revenue growth. It enables customer success teams to identify upsell and cross-sell opportunities based on customer usage data and behavioral patterns. This data-driven approach not only increases the likelihood of successfully expanding customer accounts but also positions the organization as a trusted advisor, thereby bolstering revenue streams.

Furthermore, the automation capabilities inherent in CSM software free up valuable time for customer success professionals, allowing them to focus on strategic, high-impact initiatives rather than mundane administrative tasks. This newfound efficiency translates into cost savings and more effective resource allocation.

Best Practices for Implementing CSM Software

To implement CSM software effectively, you need to follow a few key steps:

- *Identify your customer success goals:* Before selecting a CSM tool, you need to understand your customer success goals. Are you looking to reduce churn, increase upsell/cross-sell opportunities, improve customer satisfaction, or all of the above? Understanding your goals will help you select a CSM tool that aligns with your objectives.

- *Select the right CSM software:* Once you've identified your goals, it's time to select the best CSM software for your business. There are several options available in the market, each with its unique features and benefits. Make sure you evaluate your options carefully before making a decision.

- *Customize the software to meet your needs:* Once you've selected your CSM software, it's important to customize it to meet your specific needs. This may involve creating custom fields, setting up workflows, and integrating the tool with other software systems.

- *Train your team:* To ensure successful adoption of CSM software, you need to train your team on how to use the tool effectively. Make sure your team understands the software's features and benefits and how to use it to achieve your customer success goals.

Metrics to Measure Success

- *Customer satisfaction:* CSM software can help you track CSAT levels, enabling you to identify areas where you need to improve.
- *Churn rate:* By tracking churn rate, you can identify areas where you need to focus on improving customer retention.
- *Upsell/cross-sell opportunities:* CSM software can help you track upsell and cross-sell opportunities, allowing the business to create product pipelines and forecasting reports. These can be used over time to show revenue success from the customer success department.
- *Time to resolution:* By tracking the time it takes to resolve customer issues, you can identify areas where you need to improve your processes and procedures.

Real-World Examples

Adobe

One of Adobe's key goals was to reduce churn and enhance customer satisfaction. To achieve this, the company utilized CSM software to create highly personalized onboarding experiences for new customers. Adobe recognized that the early stages of a customer's journey are pivotal in shaping their perception of the product and the company as a whole. With CSM software, Adobe was able to collect and analyze data on customer behavior, preferences, and engagement patterns.

Adobe then used these insights to develop tailored onboarding processes for different customer segments. For instance, it identified that some customers required in-depth training on advanced features while others needed a more streamlined onboarding experience. CSM software enabled Adobe to automate the delivery of customized content, tutorials, and resources to meet the specific needs of each customer group.

As a result, new customers felt supported and empowered from day one, reducing the likelihood of churn. Adobe also used the software to proactively identify potential issues during the onboarding process and address them promptly. This approach not only increased customer satisfaction but also created a strong foundation for long-term relationships, setting the stage for potential upsell opportunities.

Why Using CSM Software Aids Customer Retention

Implementing CSM software can be a game-changer when it comes to retaining customers and fostering long-lasting relationships. It's a multifaceted toolkit that empowers customer success teams to proactively engage with customers, understand their needs, and deliver exceptional experiences.

CSM software acts as a central hub for customer data and interactions. It enables customer success teams to collect and store valuable information about each customer, including their preferences, challenges, and engagement history. This comprehensive customer profile serves as the foundation for personalized interactions. When customers feel understood and valued, they are more likely to stay loyal to a company.

Secondly, CSM software facilitates proactive communication and engagement. It can automate processes like onboarding, check-ins, and follow-ups, ensuring that customers receive timely support and guidance. For example, if a customer hasn't engaged with a product feature in a while, the software can trigger automated messages with tips and resources to encourage usage. This level of proactivity prevents customers from feeling neglected and addresses their needs before they become issues that lead to churn.

How CSM Software Can Improve Upsell and Cross-Sell Opportunities

Customer success management software has become an indispensable tool for businesses as it helps them enhance and make the most of their upsell and cross-sell opportunities.

Firstly, CSM software allows companies to gain a comprehensive understanding of their customers' needs and behaviors. By tracking customer interactions and collecting data on their preferences, businesses can identify the right moments to suggest additional products or services that align with the customer's existing purchases. This proactive approach helps in creating personalized offers and recommendations, increasing the likelihood of upselling or cross-selling successfully.

Moreover, CSM software enables companies to segment their customer base effectively, allowing for tailored marketing campaigns that address the specific needs and pain points of each segment. This targeted approach maximizes the success of upsell and cross-sell initiatives.

CSM software also empowers businesses to automate and streamline their customer engagement processes. Through the use of automated alerts and triggers, companies can react swiftly to customer behavior or feedback. For example, if a customer shows increased engagement with a particular product, the software can automatically trigger a notification for the sales team to reach out with complementary offerings. This real-time responsiveness ensures that upsell and cross-sell opportunities are seized promptly, preventing them from slipping through the cracks.

Additionally, CSM software often includes analytics and reporting features, which enable businesses to measure the success of their upsell and cross-sell strategies. By tracking key performance indicators (KPIs) and evaluating the effectiveness of various approaches, companies can continually refine their tactics, leading to improved customer satisfaction and revenue growth. In this way, CSM software becomes an invaluable asset for driving upsell and cross-sell opportunities in today's competitive market.

Final Thoughts

In the current landscape of intense business competition, customer success management software has become a crucial asset for companies aiming to enhance customer contentment and loyalty and their upselling and cross-selling success rates.

This software grants companies deeper insights into customer requirements and inclinations. Moreover, it helps pinpoint areas that require service enhancement. In this manner, CSM software not only enables companies to maintain a competitive edge but also enables them to provide unparalleled customer experiences.

Chapter Thirty-Four
Customer Relationship Management and Marketing Automation Integration

Integrating customer relationship management (CRM) and marketing automation systems can streamline customer success processes and help organizations achieve their customer retention, upsell, and cross-sell goals.

In this chapter, we will explore the benefits of CRM and marketing automation integration, techniques for implementation, metrics to measure success, real-world examples, and the potential impact on customer retention and growth.

Why CRM and Marketing Automation Matter

Integrating CRM and marketing automation systems represents a pivotal step in optimizing customer success processes within an organization. Synergy between these two critical systems yields a range of benefits that significantly contribute to achieving key objectives such as customer retention, upselling, and cross-selling.

Integrating these tools facilitates a comprehensive view of customer data. CRM systems centralize vital customer information, including contact details, purchase history, and interaction logs. When connected to marketing automation systems, this data is enriched with insights from marketing campaigns, website visits, and email interactions. The result is a 360-degree customer profile that equips customer success teams with a deep understanding of each customer's behavior, preferences, and engagement history. Armed with this holistic view, teams can personalize interactions and address specific needs and concerns, ultimately enhancing customer satisfaction and retention.

Secondly, this integration streamlines communication and engagement. Marketing automation tools enable personalized, timely, and relevant customer communications to be automated. By linking these tools with CRM systems, customer success teams can trigger automated messages or nurture campaigns based on customer behaviors or milestones, such as completing a purchase or renewing a subscription. This ensures consistent and targeted communication, reinforcing customer relationships and increasing the likelihood of upsell or cross-sell opportunities.

Lead management and conversion tracking are enhanced with CRM and marketing automation systems. CRM systems are adept at managing leads, tracking sales opportunities, and monitoring the sales pipeline. When aligned with marketing automation, this capability extends to tracking leads generated from marketing efforts. Customer success teams can readily access information on leads, their interactions with marketing materials, and their progression through the sales funnel. This synergy enables teams to identify high-potential leads for upselling or cross-selling, making the sales process more efficient and effective.

The combination of CRM and marketing automation also aids in performance measurement and analytics. Leveraging both systems enables organizations to gain insights into the effectiveness of marketing campaigns, customer engagement strategies, and the overall customer success process. Robust reporting and analytics tools allow teams to assess which marketing initiatives are driving customer retention and upsell or cross-sell opportunities, enabling data-driven decision-making for continuous improvement.

Best Practices for Integrating CRM and Marketing Automation Tools

- *Define goals and objectives:* Clearly define the goals and objectives you would like to achieve through the integration. Determine what success looks like.

- *Evaluate CRM and marketing automation platforms:* Evaluate different platforms based on their features, pricing, and customer support. Choose platforms that meet your business needs and can seamlessly integrate with each other.

- *Train teams:* Provide comprehensive training to all teams involved in the integration process, including customer success, sales, marketing, and customer support. Ensure they are proficient in using the platforms and can leverage them to provide the best customer experience.

- *Develop automated workflows:* Develop automated workflows that will guide customers through the customer journey, from the initial contact to post-sale support. These workflows should be optimized to provide personalized experiences to customers and drive upsell and cross-sell opportunities.

- *Analyze data:* Analyze data from both CRM and marketing automation platforms to identify trends and patterns in customer behavior. This analysis can help customer success teams identify potential opportunities for upselling and cross-selling.

- *Test and refine:* Continuously test and refine the integration to ensure it is meeting the goals and objectives you set at the beginning. Make necessary adjustments to the workflows and processes to ensure the integration is driving the desired outcomes.

Metrics to Measure

- *Lead conversion rate:* The percentage of leads that convert into paying customers.
- *Customer retention rate:* The percentage of customers who continue to use your product or service over a given period of time.
- *Customer lifetime value (CLV):* The total amount of revenue a customer is expected to generate over the course of their relationship with the company.
- *Sales cycle length:* The amount of time it takes for a lead to convert into a paying customer.
- *Net promoter score (NPS):* A metric that measures customer satisfaction and loyalty.

Real-World Examples

- *Salesforce's integration with Pardot:* Salesforce is a CRM platform that allows businesses to manage customer relationships and sales, while Pardot is a marketing automation platform that automates lead-generation and lead-nurturing processes. The integration allows businesses to create targeted marketing campaigns and track leads through the sales funnel, resulting in increased lead conversion rates and sales.

- *HubSpot's CRM and marketing automation platform:* HubSpot's CRM platform allows businesses to manage customer relationships and sales, while its marketing automation platform automates lead generation and lead nurturing processes. The integration provides businesses with a single source of truth for customer data, resulting in a more personalized and streamlined customer experience.

Why Integrating CRM and Marketing Automation Aids Customer Retention

The integration of CRM and marketing automation provides a personalized and streamlined customer experience, which boosts customer retention. By integrating customer data from both platforms, businesses can also provide a more personalized experience to customers. This can lead to increased customer satisfaction and loyalty, resulting in higher customer retention rates.

How This Strategy Can Improve Upsell and Cross-sell Opportunities

By analyzing data from both platforms, customer success teams can identify potential opportunities for upselling and cross-selling. This can help businesses increase revenue from existing customers and improve their overall customer lifetime value.

Final Thoughts

The integration of CRM and marketing automation systems is a game-changer for customer success strategies. It offers a multitude of advantages, including a comprehensive view of customer data, streamlined communication, efficient lead management, and data-driven decision-making. This synergy equips customer success teams with the tools and insights they need to excel in retaining customers, driving upsell and cross-sell opportunities, and fostering overall growth.

By combining CRM and marketing automation, organizations can personalize interactions, address specific customer needs, and boost satisfaction and loyalty. The integration enables consistent, targeted communication that reinforces relationships and increases the chances of upsell or cross-sell success. Moreover, lead management becomes more efficient, with high-potential leads readily identified for further engagement.

Performance measurement and analytics are also elevated through this integration, allowing businesses to continually refine their strategies and make data-driven decisions. By closely monitoring lead conversion rates, customer retention, customer lifetime value, sales cycle length, and net promoter scores, organizations can fine-tune their approaches to maximize results.

Ultimately, integrating CRM and marketing automation is a strategy that combines data-driven precision with personalized customer interactions, resulting in stronger, more profitable customer relationships and sustainable growth.

Part VII: Engagement and Team Building

"Coming together is a beginning. Keeping together is progress. Working together is success." — Henry Ford, founder of Ford Motor Company

Chapter Thirty-Five
Personalization and Customization

In many customer success departments, personalization and customization have emerged as key strategies for delivering exceptional customer experiences.

This chapter explores the importance of personalization and customization in customer success, provides techniques to implement these strategies effectively, suggests metrics to measure success, shares real-world examples from leading companies, and discusses how this strategy improves customer retention and drives upsell and cross-sell opportunities.

Why Personalization and Customization Matter

Personalization and customization are no longer just optional strategies for customer success teams in enterprise companies; they are fundamental pillars upon which successful customer relationships are built. These twin concepts are instrumental in creating experiences that resonate deeply with individual customers, forging bonds that endure and drive long-term loyalty.

At the core of personalization and customization lies a profound shift in how companies approach their interactions with customers. They signify a departure from one-size-fits-all approaches and a shift to a commitment to understanding each customer's unique needs, preferences, and expectations. This transformation encompasses every facet of customer engagement, from tailored product recommendations and personalized marketing communications to customized support experiences.

One key dimension of personalization and customization is the use of customer data. By harnessing the wealth of data available today, such as purchase history, browsing behavior, and demographic information, customer success teams can craft highly personalized journeys. For instance, an e-commerce platform might use past purchase data to recommend products that align with a customer's previous buying patterns. Similarly, content recommendation engines can leverage browsing history to suggest articles or videos that resonate with an individual's interests.

Effective personalization and customization extend beyond the digital realm. They manifest in the way support is provided, with customer service representatives armed with a comprehensive view of a customer's history and specific issues. This enables a more empathetic and efficient resolution process. These approaches also extend to the design and configuration of products or services, allowing customers to tailor their experiences according to their preferences. This empowerment enhances customer satisfaction and fosters a sense of ownership over the product or service.

Perhaps the most significant impact of personalization and customization is on the overall customer experience. When customers believe that a company understands their unique needs and tries its best to cater to them, it engenders a sense of being valued and heard. This, in turn, contributes significantly to customer satisfaction and loyalty. Personalized experiences are memorable, and they often result in customers becoming advocates for the brand, promoting it to others through word of mouth and referrals.

However, achieving effective personalization and customization necessitates a robust technological infrastructure. Companies need systems capable of aggregating and analyzing customer data in real time, as well as platforms that can deliver personalized content, recommendations, and support. The development of comprehensive customer profiles powered by artificial intelligence and machine learning is increasingly pivotal in this endeavor.

Best Practices for Implementing Personalization and Customization

- *Customer profiling:* Develop detailed customer profiles that capture essential information about their demographics, preferences, goals, and pain points. This data will serve as the foundation of personalized interactions.
- *Dynamic content and messaging:* Utilize marketing automation and customer relationship management (CRM) systems to deliver targeted and relevant content to customers based on their interests, behaviors, and progression through the customer journey.
- *Tailored solutions and recommendations:* Leverage customer data and analytics to provide customized solutions that address specific customer needs. Proactively recommend products or features that align with your customers' goals and deliver value.

- *Adaptive customer communications:* Adapt communication channels and styles based on customer preferences. Some customers may prefer email, while others may prefer phone calls or live chat. Offer flexibility and ensure consistent communication across channels.

Metrics to Measure

- *Personalization effectiveness:* Measure the impact of personalization efforts on customer satisfaction, engagement, and loyalty. Track metrics such as customer feedback scores, net promoter scores (NPS), and customer sentiment.
- *Conversion rates:* Evaluate the conversion rates of personalized offers, recommendations, and cross-sell/upsell initiatives. Measure the percentage of customers who have responded positively to personalized communications and made additional purchases.
- *Customer lifetime value (CLV):* Analyze the CLV of customers who have experienced personalized interactions compared to those who have not. Measure the long-term revenue generated by customers who have received personalized treatment.

Real-World Examples

- *Amazon:* Amazon uses sophisticated algorithms to personalize product recommendations based on a customer's browsing and purchasing history. This personalized approach enhances the customer's shopping experience and increases their likelihood of making repeat purchases.

- *Spotify:* Spotify's Discover Weekly feature uses personalized algorithms to curate a unique playlist for each user based on their music preferences and listening habits. This tailored experience keeps users engaged and encourages them to continue using the platform.

Why Personalization and Customization Aid Customer Retention

Personalization and customization create a sense of individual attention and care, making customers feel valued and understood. By tailoring interactions and solutions to customers' specific needs, customer success teams can enhance satisfaction, build trust, and foster long-term relationships. This strategy demonstrates a commitment to meeting customers' unique requirements, resulting in increased loyalty and reduced churn.

How Personalization and Customization Can Improve Upsell and Cross-Sell Opportunities

Personalization and customization provide an opportunity to identify upsell and cross-sell opportunities by revealing customers' pain points and goals. By leveraging personalized recommendations and tailored solutions, customer success teams can effectively position additional products or services that address customers' evolving needs. This approach increases the likelihood of successful upsells and cross-sells, driving revenue growth.

Final Thoughts

In the competitive landscape of enterprise customer success, personalization and customization have emerged as critical strategies for driving customer satisfaction, retention, and revenue growth.

When they follow best practices, such as using customer profiling, delivering dynamic content, providing tailored solutions, and offering adaptive communication, customer success teams can create personalized experiences that resonate with customers on a deeper level.

Metrics such as personalization effectiveness, conversion rates, and CLV equip organizations with the insights they need to assess the success of their personalization efforts and make data-driven improvements.

Chapter Thirty-Six
Agile Development Methodologies

In this chapter, we will explore how enterprise companies can effectively utilize Agile development methodologies in their customer success strategies. By adopting Agile principles and practices, customer success teams can enhance their responsiveness, adaptability, and collaboration, resulting in improved customer satisfaction and retention. We will discuss techniques for implementing Agile in customer success, metrics to measure its effectiveness, real-world examples from leading companies, and the impact of Agile on upsell and cross-sell opportunities.

What are Agile Development Methodologies?

An Agile development methodology is an iterative and incremental approach to software development that prioritizes flexibility, collaboration, and customer-centricity. Instead of following a rigid, linear process, Agile breaks projects into smaller, manageable tasks or "sprints." Each sprint typically lasts a few weeks and involves a cross-functional team working together to deliver a specific set of features or functionalities. At the end of each sprint, the team reviews the progress, gathers feedback, and makes adjustments based on customer needs and changing requirements.

This iterative process allows for continuous improvement and enables the team to respond quickly to evolving priorities and challenges.

Agile Development Methodologies in Customer Success

Although Agile values originate from the realm of software development, customer success teams can also employ Agile principles and methodologies to help achieve their goals in various ways.

Firstly, by adopting an Agile mindset, the customer success team can become more responsive and adaptable to customers' changing needs and expectations. The iterative nature of Agile allows the team to regularly assess and reassess their strategies and approaches, making real-time adjustments to better support customers and achieve their desired outcomes.

Agile also promotes regular and transparent communication between the customer success team and their customers. By involving customers in sprint reviews and feedback sessions, the team can gain valuable insights into the effectiveness of their support efforts and identify areas for improvement. This customer engagement fosters a collaborative relationship, where customers feel empowered to actively participate in the success of their own journey.

Moreover, Agile enables the customer success team to prioritize tasks based on customer needs and feedback. By breaking down larger objectives into smaller, actionable tasks, the team can focus on addressing the most critical customer pain points first, ensuring that resources are efficiently utilized to maximize customer value.

The Agile approach also encourages experimentation and innovation. The customer success team can try out new strategies in a controlled environment and gather data to assess their impact on customer satisfaction and success. This experimentation-driven approach allows the team to continuously refine and optimize their practices.

Best Practices for Implementing Agile in Customer Success

- *Cross-functional teams:* Forming cross-functional teams consisting of customer success managers, product specialists, and technical experts ensures streamlined communication and collaboration, enabling quick responses to customer needs.
- *Iterative planning:* Break down customer success initiatives into manageable tasks and prioritize them based on customer impact. Use short iterations and regular checkpoints to track progress and adapt strategies as needed.
- *Continuous improvement:* Embrace a culture of continuous improvement by regularly reviewing and reflecting on customer success processes, soliciting customer feedback, and implementing changes to enhance value delivery.
- *Agile tools:* Utilize Agile project management tools, such as Kanban boards or Scrum boards, to visualize tasks, track progress, and promote transparency and accountability within the team.

Metrics to Measure

- *Time to value:* Measure the time it takes to deliver value to customers, from onboarding to achieving desired outcomes. Decreasing the time to value indicates improved efficiency and customer satisfaction.

- *Customer satisfaction (CSAT) score:* Assess customer satisfaction through surveys or feedback mechanisms. Agile practices should result in higher CSAT scores due to faster response times, continuous improvement, and tailored solutions.

- *Customer retention rate:* Monitor the percentage of customers who renew their contracts or continue using the product/service. Agile methodologies can contribute to higher customer retention rates by proactively addressing customer needs.

- *Customer success velocity:* Measure the speed at which customer success teams resolve customer issues or deliver value. Agile practices should enhance customer success velocity by enabling faster decision-making and problem-solving.

Real-World Examples

- *Spotify:* Spotify's customer success teams employ Agile methodologies to continuously enhance the user experience. By implementing regular iterations, gathering user feedback, and quickly iterating on the product, Spotify ensures high customer satisfaction and retention.

- *Salesforce:* Salesforce uses Agile methodologies to deliver frequent updates and new features to its customers. By embracing Agile, Salesforce maintains a competitive edge and keeps customers engaged with the platform.

Why Agile Development Methodologies Aid Customer Retention

Agile development methodologies align with the dynamic nature of customer expectations. By prioritizing customer needs, embracing flexibility, and fostering collaboration, Agile enables customer success teams to provide timely and tailored solutions. This customer-centric approach strengthens relationships, improves customer satisfaction, and ultimately leads to higher retention rates.

How Agile Development Methodologies Improve Upsell and Cross-Sell Opportunities

Agile methodologies empower customer success teams to adapt quickly to changing customer requirements and market trends. This agility enables teams to identify upsell and cross-sell opportunities based on real-time customer feedback and evolving needs.

By delivering value incrementally and continuously improving their offerings, organizations can enhance upsell and cross-sell success rates and drive revenue growth.

Final Thoughts

Incorporating Agile development methodologies in customer success is essential for enterprise companies seeking to deliver exceptional customer experiences, improve retention rates, and drive upsell and cross-sell opportunities.

By implementing Agile techniques, measuring relevant metrics, and learning from real-world examples, organizations can foster a customer-centric culture, adapt to customer needs rapidly, and achieve sustainable growth in today's competitive business landscape.

Chapter Thirty-Seven
DevOps and Continuous Delivery

Client success teams in enterprise companies must embrace DevOps and continuous delivery (CD) practices to enhance customer satisfaction, improve product quality, and drive business growth — especially in today's fast-based business environment.

This chapter explores the importance of DevOps and CD in customer success, recommends best practices to follow, suggests metrics to measure, and offers real-world examples and insights into how this strategy can help your organization retain customers and boost upsell and cross-sell opportunities.

These practices are not merely technological trends. They represent a fundamental shift in how organizations operate, aligning seamlessly with the overarching goal of enhancing customer satisfaction, improving product quality, and, ultimately, driving business growth.

What Do We Mean by DevOps and Continuous Delivery?

DevOps, at its core, is a cultural and operational philosophy that seeks to bridge the traditional divide between development and operations teams. It emphasizes collaboration, automation, and a continuous feedback loop throughout the software development lifecycle. By adopting DevOps principles, customer success teams can enjoy several transformative benefits.

First and foremost, DevOps fosters agility and speed in the delivery of software updates and new features. In a rapidly evolving business environment, being able to respond swiftly to customer needs and market changes is crucial. Continuous delivery streamlines the process of testing and deploying software, enabling customer success teams to roll out improvements and fixes more rapidly. This agility is crucial in keeping customers satisfied by addressing issues promptly and providing them with innovative solutions.

Moreover, DevOps and CD practices inherently improve product quality. Frequent, automated testing and deployment processes reduce the likelihood of introducing bugs or errors into the software. This results in a more stable and reliable product, minimizing disruptions for customers. In turn, higher product quality contributes to increased customer satisfaction, as users experience fewer issues and enjoy a smoother experience.

Another pivotal aspect of DevOps is the emphasis on continuous monitoring and feedback. Customer success teams can utilize monitoring tools to gain real-time insights into how customers are using the product and where they may be encountering challenges. This data-driven approach allows teams to proactively identify and address issues, even before customers report them. By staying ahead of potential problems, customer success teams can maintain a high level of customer satisfaction and prevent churn.

Embracing DevOps and continuous delivery practices aligns closely with the pursuit of business growth. Satisfied customers are more likely to become loyal advocates for a brand, promoting it to others through word of mouth and referrals. This organic growth is often more cost-effective and sustainable than acquiring new customers. Additionally, the ability to rapidly innovate and introduce new features can open up opportunities for upselling or cross-selling, further contributing to revenue growth.

Best Practices for Implementing DevOps and Continuous Delivery

- *Automation:* Automate the build, test, and deployment processes to eliminate manual errors and ensure consistent delivery of high-quality software.
- *Collaboration:* Foster collaboration and communication between development, operations, and customer success teams to align goals and streamline processes.
- *Infrastructure as code:* Use infrastructure automation tools to manage and provision infrastructure resources efficiently, enabling faster deployments and scalability.
- *Continuous integration and deployment:* Implement continuous integration to merge code changes frequently and continuous deployment to automatically deploy code to production environments.
- *Monitoring and feedback loops:* Establish robust monitoring and feedback mechanisms to identify and address issues proactively, improving overall system reliability and customer experience.

Metrics to Measure

- *Deployment frequency:* Measure the frequency of successful deployments to gauge the efficiency of the continuous delivery process.
- *Mean time to recovery (MTTR):* Track the time taken to recover from incidents or failures. This metric indicates the team's ability to resolve issues promptly.
- *Customer satisfaction:* Gather customer feedback on the quality and reliability of the product or service to assess CSAT levels.
- *Time to value:* Measure the time it takes for customers to realize the value of the product or service, reflecting the effectiveness of the CD approach.
- *Release stability:* Monitor the number of bugs or incidents introduced with each release to evaluate the product's stability.

Real-World Examples

- *Amazon:* Amazon's DevOps and continuous delivery practices allow the company to frequently release new features and updates to its online marketplace, ensuring a seamless customer experience.
- *Netflix:* Netflix leverages DevOps and continuous delivery to deliver a reliable streaming service, rapidly roll out new content, and personalize recommendations for millions of users.

- *Spotify:* Spotify's customer success teams utilize DevOps and continuous delivery to deliver a continuously evolving music streaming platform, providing an exceptional user experience and personalized playlists.

Why Implementing DevOps and Continuous Delivery Aids Customer Retention

Implementing DevOps and continuous delivery in customer success brings several benefits that contribute to customer retention.

Firstly, it enables new features, enhancements, and bug fixes to be delivered more quickly, addressing customer needs and reducing time to value. Additionally, the proactive monitoring and feedback loops allow for early detection and resolution of issues, ensuring a smooth and uninterrupted customer experience. The increased reliability and stability of the product or service build trust and loyalty among customers, making them less likely to churn.

How This Strategy Can Improve Upsell and Cross-Sell Opportunities

DevOps and continuous delivery facilitate faster time to market for new features, enabling customer success teams to identify upsell and cross-sell opportunities based on customer feedback and needs. The ability to rapidly introduce enhancements and tailor offerings to specific customer segments enhances upselling and cross-selling potential.

Ultimately, when customer success teams consistently deliver value and demonstrate a commitment to meeting customer requirements, they can increase revenue through expansion opportunities.

Final Thoughts

The integration of DevOps and continuous delivery practices is a strategic imperative for customer success teams in enterprise companies. These practices empower teams to enhance customer satisfaction by delivering higher-quality products more quickly while also fostering a culture of continuous improvement and innovation.

In today's fast-paced business environment, the ability to adapt and excel in this manner is not just a competitive advantage; it's a requirement for sustained success and growth.

Chapter Thirty-Eight
Community Building and Engagement

In today's business landscape, fostering a strong community around your product or service is crucial for customer success in enterprise companies. This chapter will explore the importance of community building and engagement, best practices for implementing these approaches, metrics that enable you to measure their effects, real-world examples, and how this strategy can boost upsell and cross-sell opportunities. By the end, you'll see how leveraging the power of community allows customer success teams to drive customer satisfaction, retention, and business growth.

Why Community Building and Engagement Matter

A customer community can be a powerful tool that supports customer success goals by fostering engagement, collaboration, and knowledge sharing among customers. Creating a dedicated online platform for customers to connect, ask questions, share best practices, and provide feedback means companies can facilitate a sense of belonging and ownership within their customer base. Community members can offer valuable insights, solutions, and peer-to-peer support, enhancing overall customer satisfaction and product adoption. Additionally, the community can act as a knowledge and resource repository, empowering customers to become more proficient at using the product or service and see better results.

The customer success team can actively participate in the community, responding to inquiries, addressing concerns, and providing valuable guidance. The team can identify emerging trends, pain points, and opportunities for improvement when they actively monitor community interactions. Engaging with customers in the community also reinforces the company's commitment to their success, building trust and loyalty.

Ultimately, a well-managed customer community becomes a collaborative hub that not only supports customer success goals but also creates a vibrant ecosystem where customers feel valued, connected, and empowered to achieve their desired outcomes.

Best Practices for Community Building and Engagement

- *Establish a community platform:* Create a dedicated online platform, such as a forum or social media group, where customers can connect, share insights, and seek support.
- *Encourage active participation:* Promote engagement within the community by posing questions, sharing helpful content, and facilitating discussions.
- *Host events and webinars:* Organize virtual or in-person events where customers can network, learn from industry experts, and share best practices.

- *Recognize and reward contributors:* Acknowledge and appreciate community members who actively contribute by offering incentives, badges, or exclusive perks.

- *Facilitate peer-to-peer support:* Encourage customers to assist each other by providing guidance, sharing experiences, and solving problems together.

Metrics to Measure

- *Community growth:* Track the number of community members, active users, and new registrations to gauge the community's reach and engagement.

- *Engagement levels:* Monitor metrics such as the number of posts, comments, likes, and shares to assess the level of interaction within the community.

- *Knowledge sharing:* Measure the quantity and quality of information exchanged, including user-generated content, best practices, and success stories.

- *Customer satisfaction:* Conduct surveys or sentiment analysis to gauge customer satisfaction and perceptions of the community's value.

- *Retention and advocacy:* Evaluate the impact of the community on customer retention and advocacy by tracking renewal rates and referral rates.

Real-World Examples

- *Salesforce Trailblazer Community:* Salesforce's community platform allows users to connect, collaborate, and learn from each other, fostering a sense of belonging and driving customer success.
- *HubSpot User Groups:* HubSpot organizes regional user groups and virtual events where customers can network, gain product knowledge, and share their expertise.
- *Airbnb Host Community Center:* Airbnb provides a dedicated platform for hosts where they can connect, access resources, ask questions, and learn from other hosts and those who are more experienced.

Why Community Building and Engagement Aids Customer Retention

Building a community creates a sense of belonging and connection among customers. It allows them to engage with like-minded individuals, share experiences, and seek support. This sense of community enhances customer satisfaction, loyalty, and, ultimately, retention. Customers who feel like they are part of a community are more likely to remain engaged with the brand, seek answers to their questions instead of churning, and become brand advocates.

How Community Building and Engagement Can Improve Upsell and Cross-Sell Opportunities

A strong community fosters trust, credibility, and loyalty among its members. By actively engaging with the community, customer success teams can identify customers who are primed for upsell and cross-sell opportunities. These engaged customers will be more receptive to product recommendations, upgrades, or additional services, leading to increased upsell and cross-sell conversions.

Final Thoughts

Community building and engagement play a vital role in customer success for enterprise companies. Creating a dedicated community platform, encouraging active participation, hosting events, recognizing contributors, and facilitating peer-to-peer support enables customer success teams to foster a vibrant and supportive community.

Measuring key metrics like community growth, engagement levels, knowledge sharing, customer satisfaction, retention, and advocacy provides valuable insights into the community's success and overall impact. Well-known companies like Salesforce, HubSpot, and Airbnb rely on these approaches, and these examples demonstrate the effectiveness of community-building strategies in enhancing customer satisfaction, retention, and advocacy.

Community building is directly correlated with upsell and cross-sell opportunities. Engaged community members are more likely to be receptive to product recommendations and upgrades, leading to increased revenue and business growth.

Ultimately, leveraging the power of community building and engagement enables customer success teams to create a strong customer support network, foster customer loyalty, and drive business success. By following the best practices mentioned in this chapter, tracking relevant metrics, and drawing inspiration from real-world examples, enterprises can build thriving communities that enhance customer success and fuel growth.

Part VIII: Team Development and Culture

"Culture is not just one aspect of the game — it is the game." — Lou Gerstner, CEO IBM

Chapter Thirty-Nine

Leveraging an Effective Customer Success Team Structure and Roles

In this chapter, we will explore the importance of ensuring the structure and roles within a customer success team are well-defined. We will discuss the key components of an effective team structure, how to design one, metrics to measure success, and real-world examples from leading companies. We'll also look at how the structure of your customer success team can influence customer retention and upsell and cross-sell opportunities.

What Does an Effective Customer Success Team Structure Look Like?

The success of enterprise companies relies heavily on nurturing strong and long-lasting relationships with customers. A well-structured customer success team plays a pivotal role in achieving this goal. Organizations can meet customer needs effectively, drive satisfaction, and maximize revenue growth by aligning the right roles and responsibilities.

The ideal customer success team structure and the roles it includes can vary depending on the size and complexity of the organization as well as the customer base's specific needs. However, a typical structure may include the following roles:

- *Customer success manager (CSM):* CSMs are the main point of contact for individual customers. They build strong relationships with customers, understand their needs and goals, and act as advocates for their success. CSMs are responsible for onboarding new customers, providing ongoing support, and ensuring that customers derive maximum value from the product or service.

- *Customer success specialist/associate:* These team members assist CSMs in managing day-to-day interactions with customers. They may handle routine inquiries, resolve issues, and conduct regular check-ins with customers to ensure satisfaction and optimized usage.

- *Technical account manager (TAM):* For companies with technically complex products, TAMs provide specialized technical expertise and support to customers. They help with product integration, troubleshooting, and addressing technical challenges.

- *Renewals specialist:* Renewals specialists focus on contract renewals and upselling opportunities. They proactively engage with customers nearing their contract expiration, take steps to understand their needs, and negotiate renewal terms.

- *Customer success operations:* This role is responsible for managing and analyzing customer success data, tracking key performance metrics, and generating reports to measure team performance and customer health.

- *Customer success enablement/training:* These team members focus on educating customers about the product or service, offering training sessions, webinars, and self-help resources to improve product adoption and customer proficiency.

- *Customer success leadership:* This group oversees the entire customer success team, sets strategic goals, and aligns customer success initiatives with the overall company vision. Customer success leaders act as mentors and provide guidance to the rest of the team.

Communication between team members should be prioritized in an ideal team structure, fostering a cohesive and customer-centric approach. Each role plays a crucial part in driving customer success, retention, and growth, ensuring that customers receive personalized support and guidance throughout their journey. Additionally, ongoing training and development opportunities should be provided to the team so they can stay up to date with industry trends and best practices, enabling them to continuously improve and optimize the customer experience.

Designing an Effective Customer Success Team Structure

- *Defining customer success roles:* Establishing clear roles and responsibilities within the customer success team ensures a streamlined workflow and effective service delivery.
- *Building cross-functional collaboration:* Encouraging collaboration between customer success, sales, marketing, and product teams fosters a holistic approach to customer satisfaction.

- *Implementing scalable team structures:* Team structures should be designed so that the team can scale up as the organization grows. Bear in mind that the team will need to maintain efficient customer support throughout this process.

Metrics to Measure

- *Customer satisfaction (CSAT) scores and net promoter scores (NPS):* Tracking CSAT and NPS metrics provides insights into customer sentiment and the likelihood of customers recommending the organization's products or services.
- *Customer retention rate:* Measuring the percentage of customers retained over a specific period helps evaluate the effectiveness of the customer success strategy.
- *Expansion and upsell revenue:* Monitoring the revenue generated from upsells and cross-sells showcases the success of customer success efforts in driving additional business.

Real-World Examples

- *Salesforce:* Salesforce's customer success team employs a comprehensive structure consisting of CMSs, technical consultants, and support professionals. This structure ensures seamless customer onboarding, ongoing support, and upsell opportunities.
- *HubSpot:* HubSpot utilizes a collaborative team approach, with CSMs working closely with sales, marketing, and support

teams. This alignment enables them to provide personalized solutions and drive customer growth.

An Effective Customer Success Team Structure: Key to Customer Retention and Upsell and Cross-Sell Opportunities

A well-structured and strategically organized customer success team plays a crucial role in retaining customers and capitalizing on upsell and cross-sell opportunities. This is because an effective team setup ensures that customers receive personalized attention and support throughout their journey. With clear roles and responsibilities, team members can proactively address customer needs, resolve issues, and anticipate challenges, resulting in higher customer satisfaction and loyalty.

Ultimately, a well-structured customer success team creates a win-win situation: customers receive exceptional value and service, while the business sees increased revenue growth through upselling and cross-selling endeavors.

Final Thoughts

As we've explored in this chapter, a well-defined customer success team structure serves as the backbone of your organization's customer-centric approach. It's the structure that ensures your customers receive the tailored support and guidance they need to succeed, which, in turn, drives customer retention, satisfaction, and growth.

Each role within your customer success team contributes uniquely to the collective goal of fostering strong, long-lasting customer relationships. All team members — including the dedicated CSMs who act as the main advocates for individual customers, the TAMs who provide specialized technical expertise, and the renewals specialists who proactively engage customers on renewal opportunities — play a vital role in your customer's journey.

Communication and collaboration among these team members are crucially important. It's through this collaboration that the true value of an effective customer success team structure shines. By sharing insights, expertise, and customer feedback, your team can continuously refine its approach, ensuring that customer needs are met promptly and effectively. Cross-functional collaboration between customer success, sales, marketing, and product teams also nurtures a holistic approach to customer satisfaction, where the entire organization aligns to support the customer's success.

Building an effective customer success team structure is not a one-time effort; it's a dynamic process that should evolve as your organization grows. Scalability is key to accommodate increased customer support requirements without sacrificing efficiency.

Providing ongoing training and development opportunities to your team is essential. This empowers them to stay at the forefront of industry trends and best practices, enabling continuous improvement and optimization of the customer experience.

To sum up, your customer success team structure is the framework upon which customer satisfaction, retention, and growth are built. It's a dynamic ecosystem where each role serves a specific purpose, and collaboration is the driving force.

As you design and refine your team structure, keep the customer at the center of your efforts. It's their success that fuels the success of your enterprise.

Chapter Forty

Performance Coaching and Development

Performance coaching and development play a critical role in driving excellence in a customer success team and achieving exceptional customer outcomes. This chapter explores how these key focuses can impact the success of an organization's customer success strategy while boosting customer retention and capitalizing on upsell and cross-sell opportunities.

What Are Performance Coaching and Development, and Why Do They Matter?

Performance coaching and development are essential components of nurturing a high-performing and effective customer success team. These practices go beyond traditional training and supervision; they encompass ongoing support, guidance, and skill enhancement tailored to each team member's needs.

In this section, we will delve into what performance coaching and development entail and why they hold significant importance for a customer success team.

Performance Coaching

Performance coaching involves a systematic and collaborative approach to helping customer success team members reach their full potential. It focuses on enhancing individual skills, knowledge, and behaviors that directly contribute to achieving exceptional customer outcomes.

Here are some key aspects of performance coaching:

- *Individualized guidance:* Performance coaching recognizes that each team member possesses unique strengths as well as things they could improve on. Coaches work closely with individuals to identify specific goals and tailor development plans accordingly.
- *Regular feedback:* Feedback is a cornerstone of performance coaching. Coaches provide constructive, actionable feedback that highlights areas of success and those that need improvement. This ongoing dialogue helps team members track their progress and make necessary adjustments.
- *Skill enhancement:* Coaching sessions are designed to target specific skills and competencies relevant to the customer success role. Whether these sessions focus on improving communication, problem-solving, or product knowledge, the overall objective is continuous skill enhancement.
- *Accountability:* Coaches hold team members accountable for their growth and development. They set clear expectations, monitor progress, and ensure that team members take ownership of their learning and improvement.

Performance Development

Performance development complements coaching by providing resources and opportunities for team members to acquire new knowledge, develop skills, and expand their capabilities. It encompasses various learning initiatives and growth-oriented activities.

Here's why performance development matters for a customer success team:

- *Adaptability:* In a rapidly changing business environment, customer success professionals must stay up to date on industry trends, technology advancements, and evolving customer needs. Development programs ensure that the team can adapt and thrive in dynamic conditions.

- *Enhanced expertise:* Providing opportunities for team members to deepen their expertise benefits both individual career growth and the organization's ability to deliver exceptional value to customers. Well-rounded professionals are better equipped to solve complex challenges and provide innovative solutions.

- *Increased engagement:* Employees who see that their organization invests in their growth are more likely to be engaged and committed to their roles. Engaged team members are more motivated to excel, resulting in improved customer interactions and outcomes.

- *Retention:* Offering development opportunities can enhance employee retention. When team members feel they can advance their careers and develop new skills within the organization, they are more likely to stay in the long term, reducing turnover and associated costs.

- *Upsell and cross-sell readiness:* A well-developed customer success team is better positioned to identify upsell and cross-sell opportunities. As team members expand their knowledge and expertise, they can recognize areas where additional products or services can provide value to existing customers.

Performance coaching and development are critical for a customer success team because they empower team members to continually improve their skills and knowledge. This, in turn, leads to exceptional customer outcomes, increased customer retention, and the ability to capitalize on upsell and cross-sell opportunities. By investing in the growth and development of your team, you are investing in the success of your customers and your organization as a whole.

Best Practices for Implementing Performance Coaching and Development

- *Skills assessment:* Begin with a comprehensive assessment of each team member's skills and competencies. This assessment forms the basis for designing coaching and development plans.
- *Individualized coaching plans:* Tailor coaching and development plans to each team member's unique needs and goals. Recognize their strengths and areas where they can improve, and work collaboratively to set clear objectives.

- *Regular feedback:* Establish a culture of continuous feedback. Encourage open and honest communication between coaches and team members. Feedback should be constructive, specific, and focused on growth.

- *Set SMART goals:* Ensure that coaching and development goals are specific, measurable, achievable, relevant, and time-bound (SMART). This framework helps team members understand expectations and track progress.

- *Coaching skills training:* Equip coaches with the necessary coaching skills. Training should cover active listening, effective questioning, and providing actionable feedback.

- *Peer coaching and mentoring programs:* Encourage peer-to-peer coaching within the team. Team members can learn from each other and share insights and best practices. Consider implementing mentoring programs where experienced team members mentor newer ones. Mentoring relationships can provide valuable guidance and career development insights.

- *Consistency:* Maintain a regular schedule for coaching sessions. Consistency ensures that team members receive ongoing support and guidance.

- *Goal alignment:* Align coaching and development goals with broader organizational objectives. This helps team members understand how their growth contributes to the company's success.

- *Resources and tools:* Provide team members with access to resources, tools, and training materials that support their development. This may include online courses, workshops, and relevant literature.

- *Track progress:* Continuously monitor and track the progress of team members in achieving their development goals. Adjust coaching plans as needed based on their performance.

- *Recognition and rewards:* Recognize and reward team members who demonstrate significant growth and improvement. Celebrating achievements can boost motivation.

- *Manager involvement:* Involve managers in the coaching and development process. Managers can provide additional guidance and support to team members.

- *Measure impact:* Use key performance indicators (KPIs) to measure the impact of coaching and development efforts. Evaluate how these initiatives contribute to improved customer outcomes, retention rates, and upsell opportunities.

- *Regular reviews:* Conduct regular reviews of coaching and development programs to assess their effectiveness. Make adjustments and refinements based on feedback and results.

- *Feedback mechanisms:* Establish mechanisms for team members to provide feedback on the coaching and development process. Their input can help refine and improve the program.

- *Continuous learning culture:* Foster a culture of continuous learning and improvement within the team. Encourage team members to take ownership of their development.

- *Documentation:* Keep records of coaching sessions, development plans, and progress. Documentation helps both coaches and team members keep track of goals and achievements.

Implementing these best practices can help create a structured and effective approach to performance coaching and development within a customer success team. It ensures that team members receive the support and guidance they need to excel in their roles and deliver exceptional customer outcomes.

Metrics to Measure

- *Customer satisfaction and net promoter score:* Measure CSAT to assess the impact of performance coaching on customer perceptions and loyalty.
- *Customer retention and churn rate:* Monitor your organization's customer retention and churn rates to evaluate the effectiveness of performance coaching in establishing customer loyalty and satisfaction.
- *Upsell and cross-sell revenue:* Calculate the revenue generated from upselling and cross-selling efforts to gauge how performance coaching impacts customer spend.
- *Individual and team performance metrics:* Monitor individual and team performance metrics to measure the effectiveness of coaching interventions. These might include metrics like adherence to customer success plans, response times, and customer health scores.

Real-World Examples

- *Salesforce:* Salesforce employs a robust performance coaching framework that includes regular performance reviews, individualized development plans, and skill-building workshops. This approach has contributed to the company's outstanding customer retention rates and consistent revenue growth.

- *Zendesk:* Zendesk provides comprehensive coaching programs to its customer success teams, focusing on improving customer communication, product knowledge, and problem-solving skills. This investment in coaching has led to improved customer satisfaction and increased cross-sell opportunities.

Why Performance Coaching and Development Aid Customer Retention

By providing focused coaching, guidance, and skill enhancement opportunities to team members, you empower them to better understand and meet your customers' evolving needs. This heightened proficiency allows the team to establish stronger relationships, anticipate challenges, and offer proactive solutions. As a result, customers feel more supported and valued, which translates into enhanced loyalty and a higher likelihood of staying with your company.

Continuous development initiatives help to equip your customer success team with the tools and knowledge needed to adapt to changing customer demands and industry trends. This adaptability ensures that they can deliver exceptional service even in dynamic situations. Furthermore, the confidence gained from skill improvement and training positively influences how your team interacts with customers, fostering trust and collaboration.

In essence, performance coaching and development not only refine the capabilities of your customer success team but also demonstrate your commitment to consistently delivering outstanding customer experiences. This commitment fosters long-term relationships and positions your company as a trusted partner in your customers' success journeys.

How Performance Coaching and Development Improve Upsell and Cross-Sell Opportunities

Performance coaching and development programs are integral to the success of customer success teams, playing a vital role in improving customer retention and capitalizing on upsell and cross-sell opportunities. These initiatives equip team members with the skills and knowledge needed to excel in their roles and deliver exceptional customer outcomes.

These programs enhance team members' product knowledge. A deep understanding of the product or service they support allows them to identify upsell and cross-sell opportunities more effectively. This comprehensive knowledge also enables team members to present the value and benefits of additional features or services to customers with confidence. Improved communication skills empower them to engage effectively with customers, uncover their needs, actively listen to their feedback, and recommend relevant upsell or cross-sell solutions.

Performance coaching fosters a customer-centric approach. It emphasizes the importance of prioritizing customer needs and delivering value — essential when identifying upsell and cross-sell opportunities. Team members trained to put the customer first are more likely to identify opportunities that are genuinely beneficial, building trust and increasing the success rate of upsells. Furthermore, these programs often incorporate data-driven insights, allowing team members to analyze customer data and metrics. By identifying trends and patterns in customer behavior, they can target upsell and cross-sell offers more strategically, enhancing the relevance and effectiveness of their recommendations.

Continuous improvement and learning are core components of these programs, ensuring team members stay updated with product developments and industry trends. This commitment to growth ensures they can spot upsell and cross-sell opportunities early and effectively.

Lastly, performance coaching and development enable team members to overcome objections and build strong customer relationships. With objection-handling skills, they can address customer concerns about upsell or cross-sell offers persuasively, highlighting their value. Building trust is crucial for customers to consider additional offerings, and well-trained team members are adept at fostering such trust.

Final Thoughts

Performance coaching and development are instrumental in optimizing the performance of customer success teams within enterprise companies.

By implementing effective coaching programs, establishing clear performance expectations, and leveraging metrics to measure performance, organizations can drive customer success, enhance customer retention, and unlock upsell and cross-sell opportunities.

Real-world examples from Salesforce and Zendesk demonstrate the positive impact of performance coaching on customer satisfaction and revenue growth. With a structured approach to coaching and a focus on continuous improvement, customer success teams can achieve outstanding results and deliver exceptional customer experiences.

Chapter Forty-One
Incentives and Bonuses

In this chapter, we will explore how the strategic use of incentives and bonuses can drive customer success within enterprise companies. We will discuss the importance of aligning incentives with desired outcomes, techniques for implementing effective incentive programs, key metrics to measure success, real-world examples from leading companies, the impact of incentives on customer retention, and how this strategy can improve upsell and cross-sell opportunities.

Understanding Incentives and Bonuses

Leveraging incentives and bonuses in customer success involves using various rewards and recognition mechanisms to motivate and incentivize the customer success team to achieve specific performance goals and objectives. These incentives are designed to align the team's efforts with the company's strategic priorities, focusing on enhancing customer satisfaction, retention, upsell efforts, and overall revenue growth.

Incentives and bonuses can take different forms, such as:

- *Performance-based bonuses:* These are monetary rewards tied to KPIs like customer retention rates, CSAT scores, and upselling metrics. For example, a customer success manager may receive a bonus for achieving a high customer retention rate or successfully upselling to a certain percentage of customers.

- *Goal attainment bonuses:* Team members can be rewarded for achieving specific milestones or targets. Examples include successfully onboarding a certain number of new customers within a designated time frame and attaining a specified level of customer adoption.

- *Customer feedback recognition:* Recognizing team members who receive positive customer feedback or testimonials can foster a culture of customer-centricity and highlight outstanding performance in customer success.

- *Quarterly or annual performance awards:* These are recognition awards presented to top-performing individuals or teams for exceptional achievements in customer success throughout a specific period.

Why Incentives and Bonuses Matter

Incentives and bonuses in customer success for enterprise companies offer several benefits:

- *Performance motivation:* Incentives are a clear and tangible way to motivate the customer success team to go above and beyond in delivering exceptional service and results. They inspire employees to strive for excellence and take ownership of their customers' success.

- *Alignment with organizational goals:* By tying incentives to specific performance metrics, the company ensures the customer success team's efforts are aligned with the overall business objectives, such as revenue growth and customer retention.

- *Employee engagement and retention:* Incentives and recognition programs boost employee morale, job satisfaction, and overall engagement. Satisfied and motivated team members are more likely to stay with the company, reducing turnover and maintaining institutional knowledge.

- *Customer success focus:* Incentives reinforce the importance of prioritizing customer satisfaction and success. They encourage the team to proactively engage with customers, understand their needs, and provide tailored solutions.

- *Performance evaluation:* Incentives and bonuses provide a quantifiable way to evaluate individual and team performances, facilitating data-driven decision-making and identifying areas for improvement.

Best Practices for Offering Incentives and Bonuses

Incentive programs should be designed thoughtfully to avoid unintended consequences such as compromising service quality or facilitating short-term gains at the expense of long-term customer relationships. However, by aligning incentives with the right performance metrics and fostering a customer-centric culture, enterprise companies can effectively leverage incentives and bonuses to drive continuous improvement, increase customer satisfaction, and achieve sustainable business growth.

Follow these best practices to get the most out of incentive and bonus programs:

- *Goal-based incentives:* Design incentive programs that are aligned with specific customer success goals, such as customer retention rates, expansion revenue, or CSAT scores. Set clear and achievable targets for individuals and teams.

- *Tiered incentive structures:* Implement a tiered structure where incentives increase as customers achieve predefined milestones or levels of success. This encourages continuous improvement and motivates customers to reach higher levels of engagement.

- *Team collaboration incentives:* Foster a collaborative environment by implementing team-based incentives that reward collective achievements. Encourage collaboration among customer success managers, sales teams, and other relevant departments.

- *Performance-based bonuses:* Provide performance-based bonuses tied to individual or team performance metrics, such as meeting or exceeding revenue targets, reducing churn rates, or delivering exceptional customer satisfaction.

- *Recognition and non-monetary incentives:* In addition to financial rewards, implement recognition programs that acknowledge outstanding performance. Non-monetary incentives can include public recognition, career advancement opportunities, professional development resources, and special perks.

Metrics to Measure

- *Revenue growth:* Measure the impact of incentives and bonuses on overall revenue growth, including expansion revenue, upsells, and cross-sells.
- *Customer retention:* Monitor the effect of incentive programs on customer retention rates. Track churn rates and customer renewal rates to evaluate the success of the initiatives.
- *Customer satisfaction:* Assess CSAT scores and feedback to gauge the effectiveness of incentive programs in driving positive customer experiences.
- *Employee engagement:* Measure employee engagement and satisfaction levels to determine how incentives are impacting employee morale and motivation.

Real-World Examples

- *Amazon:* Amazon offers a "Pay to Quit" program where employees are given a bonus if they decide to leave the company. This incentive encourages employees who are not fully committed to the company's values and goals to voluntarily exit, leaving a workforce more dedicated to the company's success.
- *HubSpot:* HubSpot provides a culture of recognition and rewards through its "Culture Code" initiative. The company offers non-monetary incentives, such as flexible work hours, professional development opportunities, and recognition

through peer-to-peer feedback. This approach fosters a positive work environment and motivates employees to deliver exceptional customer success.

Why Incentives and Bonuses Aid Customer Retention

Introducing incentives and bonuses enables you to create a compelling incentive structure that encourages your customer success team to go above and beyond to ensure customer satisfaction. This added motivation drives team members to proactively address customer needs, resolve issues promptly, and consistently exceed expectations. As a direct result, customers feel a heightened sense of value and care, which results in their loyalty and prolonged engagement with your services.

Incentives and bonuses not only boost individual and team performances but also foster a culture of excellence and customer-centricity. When employees know that their efforts are recognized and rewarded, they are more likely to invest their energy in building strong customer relationships. Additionally, this approach aligns the interests of your customer success team with the long-term success of your customers, reinforcing a partnership mentality.

Ultimately, by leveraging incentives and bonuses, you create a win-win scenario: your customer success team is motivated to excel, leading to improved customer experiences and retention rates. This strategy underscores your commitment to delivering exceptional service and solidifies your position as a trusted partner in your enterprise customers' growth and prosperity.

How Incentives and Bonuses Can Improve Upsell and Cross-Sell Opportunities

Strategically leveraging incentives, bonuses, and commissions can be a game-changer for customer success leaders aiming to boost upsell and cross-sell results within their customer success departments. These performance-driven compensation structures serve as powerful motivators, aligning the efforts of CSMs with the organization's revenue growth and customer retention goals.

Commission-based programs are one approach. These provide a direct link between individual CSMs' success and the company's financial growth. By rewarding CSMs with commissions for successful upsell and cross-sell deals, organizations incentivize them to proactively identify opportunities within their existing customer base, encouraging them to nurture customer relationships, offer value-added solutions, and actively seek ways to expand customer engagement. As a result, CSMs become more invested in driving revenue growth.

Performance bonuses tied to specific upsell and cross-sell targets provide clear and immediate recognition for outstanding efforts. CSMs who meet or exceed these predefined goals are rewarded with performance bonuses. These bonuses serve as tangible incentives that motivate CSMs to continually identify opportunities, deliver exceptional service, and contribute to the organization's growth. By tying rewards to specific performance outcomes, leaders can ensure that CSMs remain focused on the objectives that matter most to the company.

A tiered incentive structure offers a progressive approach to motivation. CSMs can earn increasingly attractive rewards as they achieve higher goals. For example, reaching a certain upsell target might earn a CSM a bonus, but surpassing that target could result in a larger bonus or additional benefits. This tiered system encourages CSMs to continuously push their boundaries, explore larger upsell opportunities, and maintain high motivation levels throughout the year.

However, recognition and non-monetary incentives should not be underestimated. In addition to monetary rewards, acknowledging outstanding performance with public recognition, professional development opportunities, or exclusive titles can be powerful motivators. These forms of recognition foster a sense of achievement and belonging within the team, reinforcing a culture of excellence and a drive for upsell and cross-sell success.

Team-based rewards promote collaboration and teamwork within the customer success department. When the entire team collectively achieves upsell and cross-sell targets, all team members receive a shared reward. This approach nurtures a cooperative environment where team members actively support each other in identifying and capitalizing on opportunities.

Final Thoughts

Incorporating incentives and bonuses into your customer success strategy can be a powerful tool for driving customer success, retention, and revenue growth. By aligning incentives with desired outcomes, implementing effective techniques, and measuring key metrics, enterprise companies can create a culture of performance and achievement within their customer success teams.

However, it is crucial to ensure that the incentive programs are designed thoughtfully and are aligned with the organization's goals and values. Regular evaluation of metrics such as revenue growth, customer retention, customer satisfaction, and employee engagement will provide valuable insights into the effectiveness of the incentive programs and allow for necessary adjustments.

When they leverage incentives and bonuses strategically, enterprise companies can create a culture of high performance, empower their customer success teams, and, ultimately, drive long-term customer success, satisfaction, and loyalty.

Chapter Forty-Two
Gamification and Competition

In this chapter, we will explore the effective use of gamification and competition strategies within customer success teams in enterprise companies. By applying game mechanics and fostering healthy competition, organizations can drive engagement and motivation, ultimately enhancing customer success. You will discover which best practices to follow when implementing gamification and competition, the key metrics you can monitor to measure success, real-world examples from successful companies, and how this strategy contributes to retaining customers and improving upsell and cross-sell opportunities.

Why Gamification and Competition Matter

In recent times, gamification, which involves the strategic infusion of game elements into non-game contexts, has emerged as a highly effective strategy for boosting customer success.

It harnesses principles from psychology and game design to introduce elements of fun, challenges, and rewards into everyday work, reshaping the customer success experience into an engaging and dynamic endeavor. The growing popularity of gamification can be attributed to several key factors:

- *Gamification taps into intrinsic motivation and engagement.* By incorporating features such as points, badges, and leaderboards, gamification provides a sense of competition and achievement within tasks that might otherwise be routine. This intrinsic motivation keeps customer success teams motivated and encourages them to strive for excellence, resulting in improved performance.

- *Gamification offers a framework with clear objectives and immediate feedback loops.* Much like games, it defines specific goals and provides real-time feedback on progress. This clarity enables team members to understand their targets, track their advancement, and make informed decisions to enhance their outcomes.

- *This approach encourages ongoing learning and skill development.* It presents challenges, scenarios, and problem-solving tasks that require critical thinking and creativity. This not only keeps customer success teams engaged but also enhances their knowledge and proficiency in effectively addressing customer needs.

- *Collaborative teamwork is a significant benefit.* Many gamification strategies foster camaraderie and teamwork through team-based challenges and competitions. This promotes collaboration, leading to the exchange of best practices, collective problem-solving, and a stronger sense of unity within the team.

- *Gamification introduces the concept of progression and achievement.* Players in games advance through levels or stages, and this progression can be mirrored in the context of customer success to denote career growth and professional development. By linking performance milestones to promotions or tangible rewards, gamification motivates team members to continually strive for improvement.

- *Gamification provides valuable data on individual and team performance.* This data can be analyzed to gain insights into the strengths and weaknesses of customer success operations, guiding data-driven decisions to refine strategies and allocate resources more effectively.

- *Gamification's positive impact extends to the customer.* Engaged and motivated customer success teams are better equipped to provide outstanding service, resulting in heightened customer satisfaction and loyalty. Satisfied customers are more likely to remain loyal to the brand and advocate for it, contributing to overall business growth.

Best Practices for Implementing Gamification

- *Define clear objectives:* Clearly articulate the desired outcomes and behaviors you want to incentivize, such as customer satisfaction, retention, upselling, or specific performance metrics.

- *Design engaging challenges:* Create challenges that are meaningful, relevant, and aligned with organizational goals. Ensure they are challenging yet attainable to maintain motivation.

- *Reward systems:* Establish a variety of rewards, both intrinsic (like badges or recognition) and extrinsic (like monetary incentives or prizes), to cater to different motivations and preferences.

- *Progress tracking:* Implement a system to track and display individual and team progress, such as leaderboards, progress bars, or achievement milestones, to drive healthy competition.
- *Collaboration and social elements:* Foster collaboration and social interaction among team members by incorporating features like team challenges, collaborative goals, and peer recognition.

Metrics to Measure

- *Adoption and engagement:* Measure the level of participation and engagement with gamified elements, such as completion rates, points earned, and activity levels.
- *Performance metrics:* Assess the impact of gamification on KPIs such as customer satisfaction scores, retention rates, upsell/cross-sell revenue, and customer lifetime value (LTV).
- *Feedback and surveys:* Collect feedback from customers and the customer success team to evaluate the effectiveness of the gamification approach and their satisfaction with it.
- *Employee motivation and satisfaction:* Monitor employee motivation, satisfaction, and retention rates to gauge the impact of gamification on team morale and job satisfaction.

Real-World Examples

- *Salesforce Trailhead:* Salesforce's gamified learning platform encourages users to complete training modules and earn badges, fostering knowledge acquisition and engagement within the customer success community.

- *LinkedIn Sales Navigator:* LinkedIn incorporates gamification elements like leaderboards and achievement badges to incentivize sales professionals to engage with the platform, build networks, and achieve sales targets.

Why Gamification and Competition Aid Customer Retention

Gamification appeals to the intrinsic human desire for achievement, recognition, and rewards. By incorporating game mechanics such as points, levels, badges, leaderboards, and challenges, enterprises can create an environment that fosters motivation, collaboration, and continuous improvement.

Engaged and motivated customer success teams are more likely to deliver exceptional service, leading to higher customer satisfaction, loyalty, and, ultimately, retention.

How Gamification and Competition Improve Upsell and Cross-Sell Opportunities

Gamification not only impacts customer retention but also enhances upsell and cross-sell opportunities. By setting goals and milestones tied to revenue growth and expansion, organizations can incentivize customer success teams to proactively identify upsell and cross-sell opportunities. Through healthy competition and rewards, teams are motivated to explore new avenues, engage customers strategically, and drive additional value for both the customer and the company.

Final Thoughts

Gamification has proven itself as a transformative strategy in the realm of customer success by injecting elements of fun, challenge, and rewards into daily tasks. This approach not only boosts individual and team performance but also elevates customer satisfaction and loyalty.

In today's competitive business environment, gamification stands out as a powerful tool to drive performance and ensure that customer success becomes an exciting and engaging journey for all involved.

Chapter Forty-Three

Ensuring Communication and Alignment in a Customer Success Team

Effective communication and alignment within the customer success team are essential for driving customer satisfaction and retention in the fast-paced world of business.

This chapter explores the significance of ensuring there is alignment in your customer success team and that team members communicate effectively. We provide three real-life examples from well-known brands that demonstrate how customer success teams can function optimally. You will also discover how communication and alignment aid customer retention and improve upselling and cross-selling efforts. Let's dive in!

Why Do Communication and Alignment Matter in a Customer Success Team?

Effective communication and alignment within the customer success team are crucial for delivering exceptional customer experiences and ensuring long-term success. When members of the customer success team communicate seamlessly and align their efforts, the following benefits can be realized:

- *Streamlined customer experience:* When team members communicate effectively and align their actions, they can provide a consistent and seamless customer experience. This ensures that customers receive cohesive support, resulting in increased satisfaction and loyalty.

- *Proactive issue resolution:* Open communication allows the team to identify potential issues early on and address them proactively. By working together, the team can share insights, collaborate on problem-solving, and resolve issues before they escalate, leading to improved customer satisfaction.

- *Holistic understanding of customer needs:* When the customer success team communicates and aligns their efforts, they gain a comprehensive understanding of customer needs, pain points, and goals. This knowledge helps them tailor their approach and deliver personalized solutions, thereby strengthening customer relationships.

Best Practices for Ensuring Communication and Alignment

- *Cross-functional collaboration:* Foster collaboration between customer success team members and other departments, such as sales, marketing, and product. Regular meetings, shared goals, and joint initiatives encourage information sharing, ensuring that everyone is aligned and working toward a common objective.

- *Transparent communication channels:* Establish clear and open lines of communication within the team. Utilize collaboration tools, internal communication platforms, and regular team meetings to encourage knowledge sharing, provide updates, and address challenges collectively.

- *Defined roles and responsibilities:* Clearly define the roles and responsibilities of each team member to avoid overlaps or gaps in communication. When everyone understands their specific contributions, it promotes efficiency, accountability, and effective coordination. (More on this in Chapter 39.)

- *Knowledge management systems:* Implement robust knowledge management systems to capture and share customer insights, best practices, and solutions. A centralized repository of information ensures team members have access to the organization's collective knowledge. This enables them to provide consistent and informed support to customers.

Metrics to Measure

- *Frequency of team meetings:* Regular team meetings are essential for keeping everyone aligned. Track frequency and attendance to ensure that important information is consistently shared and discussed.

- *Performance metrics:* Evaluate individual and team performance against predefined goals and KPIs. Misalignment can lead to underperformance, so tracking performance metrics is crucial.

- *Alignment with customer goals:* Assess how well the customer success team aligns its actions with each customer's specific needs and goals. This alignment can be measured through customer feedback, surveys, or direct assessments.

- *Usage of team collaboration tools:* Monitor the use of collaboration tools like project management software, customer relationship management (CRM) systems, and communication platforms to ensure that team members are actively sharing information and collaborating effectively.

Real-World Examples

- *HubSpot:* HubSpot, a leading marketing automation platform, ensures effective communication and alignment through cross-functional collaboration. The customer success team collaborates closely with sales and marketing teams, ensuring a seamless handover from sales to customer onboarding. This results in a cohesive customer experience.

- *Slack:* Slack, a popular team communication platform, prioritizes communication and alignment in the customer success team. The team utilize transparent communication channels, such as dedicated team channels and integrations with other tools, to foster collaboration and information sharing. This ensures that team members stay aligned and deliver prompt and effective support to their customers.

- *Salesforce:* Salesforce, a leading CRM platform, emphasizes knowledge management systems to support effective communication and alignment in the customer success team. The internal knowledge base enables team members to access customer insights, best practices, and solutions, empowering them to provide consistent and informed assistance to customers.

Why an Aligned and Connected Customer Success Team Aids Customer Retention

Fostering effective communication and alignment within the customer success team plays a pivotal role in retaining customers, and here's why it works so well.

First and foremost, it ensures that customers receive consistent and dependable support. This is because the team is working together seamlessly. Such consistency builds a sense of trust, amplifies the overall customer experience, and diminishes the likelihood of customers exploring alternative options.

Furthermore, a well-functioning team can be proactive in identifying potential issues ahead of time. Early detection allows for swift and efficient resolutions, showing customers that their needs are promptly acknowledged and attended to. This level of responsiveness significantly contributes to customer loyalty.

Final Thoughts

Effective customer success teams maintain smooth and effective communication and align on key priorities and strategies. These characteristics are crucial for driving customer satisfaction, retention, and revenue growth in enterprise companies. Best practices like cross-functional collaboration, transparent communication channels, and knowledge management systems enable companies to ensure streamlined customer experiences, proactive issue resolution, and a holistic understanding of customer needs.

Metrics such as customer satisfaction, response time, resolution time, churn rate, and upsell/cross-sell rates provide insights into the effectiveness of the steps taken to improve communication and alignment. Real-world examples from HubSpot, Salesforce, and Slack demonstrate how these focuses can boost the customer success team's efforts.

By prioritizing communication and alignment in your customer success team, your company can build stronger relationships with customers, drive growth, and achieve long-term success.

Chapter Forty-Four

Leveraging Executive Sponsorship and Buy-In

Executive sponsorship and buy-in play a pivotal role in driving customer success within enterprise companies. This chapter explores the importance of executive sponsorship and buy-in, along with techniques to encourage and establish this. We will discuss the metrics to measure that can reveal whether executive sponsorship is positively impacting your customer success efforts, provide real-world examples of companies that have successfully implemented this approach, and highlight how it contributes to customer retention.

Why Executive Sponsorship and Buy-In Matter

Executive sponsorship and buy-in for customer success in enterprise companies are crucial for several reasons. Firstly, having support from top-level executives, such as the CEO or other C-suite leaders, signals the strategic importance of customer success within the organization. It demonstrates a commitment to customer-centricity and a recognition of the critical role customer success plays in driving business growth and profitability.

Secondly, executive buy-in fosters a culture of customer-centricity throughout the organization. When leaders prioritize customer success, it sets a precedent for all employees to prioritize customer needs and satisfaction in their roles. This customer-focused culture can lead to improved collaboration across departments, with a shared commitment to delivering exceptional customer experiences.

Crucially, executive sponsorship provides the necessary resources and budget for the customer success team to function effectively. Customer success initiatives often require investments in technology, training, and personnel. When executives are fully onboard with customer success, they are more likely to allocate the necessary resources to ensure the team's success.

Executive sponsorship can also help customer success teams gain access to key decision-makers within customer organizations. When executives at both the customer and enterprise company are engaged, it paves the way for strategic discussions and partnership opportunities that can drive customer success and satisfaction.

Driving accountability for customer success metrics and outcomes is another effect. When leaders are invested in customer success, they are more likely to set clear goals and expectations for the team and regularly review performance metrics.

Customer Success Can Fail Without Executive Buy-In

When executive sponsorship or buy-in is not agreed upon before the customer success team is established, it can lead to several challenges and potential failures in the implementation and effectiveness of customer success initiatives.

Here are some ways in which customer success can fail without executive support:

- *Lack of resources:* Without executive buy-in, the customer success team may not receive the necessary resources, budget, and personnel required to effectively support customers. This lack of resources can hinder the team's ability to deliver exceptional service, negatively impacting customer satisfaction and retention.

- *Misalignment of goals:* Without executive sponsorship, the customer success team may not be aligned with the broader business objectives and strategies. This misalignment can lead to conflicting priorities, making it challenging for the team to focus on the most critical customer success initiatives.

- *Limited authority:* Executive sponsorship gives the customer success team the authority and backing needed to drive customer-centric initiatives across the organization. Without this support, the team may struggle to gain buy-in from other departments or make necessary changes to improve the customer experience.

- *Inadequate cross-functional collaboration:* Customer success often involves collaboration with other teams, such as sales, marketing, and product development. Without executive sponsorship, it may be challenging to foster a culture of cross-functional collaboration, leading to disjointed efforts and a fragmented customer experience.

- *Difficulty in influencing change:* Customer success teams may identify areas for improvement that require changes in processes, products, or services. Without executive support, it may be difficult for the team to influence such changes and drive customer-centric improvements across the organization.

- *Lack of accountability:* Executive sponsorship helps create a culture of accountability for customer success metrics and outcomes. Without this support, there may be a lack of focus on measuring and improving customer success performance, making it challenging to identify areas that require improvement and measure the team's impact.

- *Limited customer advocacy:* Executive sponsorship often involves advocating for the voice of the customer (VoC) at the highest levels of the organization. Without this advocacy, the customer success team may struggle to champion customer needs and influence strategic decisions that positively impact customers.

Overall, without executive sponsorship or buy-in, customer success initiatives may lack the necessary support, resources, and alignment with business objectives to succeed. It is essential for executives to understand the strategic importance of customer success and be fully invested in building effective teams that can deliver exceptional experiences and drive long-term customer satisfaction and loyalty.

Best Practices for Establishing Executive Sponsorship and Buy-In

- *Leadership alignment:* Ensure that senior executives align their vision and goals with customer success initiatives. Establish regular meetings and communication channels to keep executives informed and engaged in the progress and challenges of customer success efforts.

- *Executive education:* Provide executive training and education on the importance of customer success and its impact on the organization. Help executives understand the value of investing in customer success and the long-term benefits it brings, including customer retention and revenue growth.

- *Clear communication channels:* Facilitate open lines of communication between executives and customer success teams. Regularly share customer success stories, feedback, and insights to highlight the positive impact of customer success initiatives and maintain executive engagement.

- *KPI alignment:* Align KPIs and metrics with executive sponsorship. Define and track metrics that demonstrate the impact of customer success on business outcomes, such as customer satisfaction, retention rate, upsell/cross-sell revenue, and customer lifetime value.

Metrics to Measure

- *Customer satisfaction:* Measure customer satisfaction through surveys, feedback, and net promoter scores. CSAT reflects the success of executive sponsorship in driving positive customer experiences.

- *Customer retention rate:* Monitor the percentage of customers retained over a specific period. High retention rates indicate the effectiveness of executive buy-in in ensuring long-term customer success and loyalty.

- *Upsell and cross-sell revenue:* Track the revenue generated from upselling and cross-selling efforts. This metric demonstrates how executive sponsorship can drive additional revenue streams through existing customer relationships.

Real-World Examples

- *Amazon:* Amazon's founder and former CEO, Jeff Bezos, exemplified strong executive sponsorship and buy-in for customer success. He prioritized customer-centricity throughout the organization, focusing on long-term customer satisfaction and loyalty. This approach contributed to Amazon's immense success and established the company as a customer-centric leader.

- *Salesforce:* Salesforce, a leading CRM provider, has been championing executive sponsorship and buy-in for customer success. Marc Benioff, the CEO and co-founder of Salesforce, actively advocates for customer success initiatives. His commitment to customer-centricity has shaped the company's culture and strategic decisions, leading to strong customer relationships and sustained growth.

- *Adobe:* Adobe, a multinational software company, emphasizes executive sponsorship and buy-in to drive customer success. Shantanu Narayen, the CEO of Adobe, has been instrumental in aligning the organization around customer success, resulting in innovative solutions and exceptional customer experiences.

Why Executive Sponsorship and Buy-In Aid Customer Retention

When senior executives actively support customer success initiatives, it demonstrates the organization's commitment to providing outstanding customer experiences. This commitment builds trust and loyalty among customers, increasing their likelihood of remaining with the company.

Executive buy-in also ensures that the necessary resources, both financial and human, are allocated to support customer success efforts. Adequate resources enable the implementation of proactive customer engagement strategies, personalized support, and continuous improvement initiatives, all of which contribute to higher customer retention rates.

Organizational alignment is another benefit. Executive sponsorship fosters a culture of customer-centricity and aligns teams across the organization. When all departments work together toward a common goal of customer success, it leads to smoother processes, enhanced collaboration, and, ultimately, better outcomes for customers.

How Executive Sponsorship and Buy-In Can Improve Upsell and Cross-Sell Opportunities

Executives often have access to valuable strategic insights and customer relationships. Their involvement in customer success initiatives enables them to provide guidance and support in identifying upsell and cross-sell opportunities. This strategic input enhances the effectiveness of upselling and cross-selling efforts.

Executive sponsorship also facilitates cross-functional collaboration and alignment — essential for successful upselling and cross-selling. When executives actively advocate for these initiatives, it encourages departments to work together, share customer insights, and develop cohesive strategies to generate additional revenue from existing customers.

Additionally, when senior executives actively engage with customers and prioritize their success, it enhances the perception of the company as a trusted partner. As such, executive sponsorship builds trust and strengthens relationships with customers. This trust and relationship make customers more receptive to upsell and cross-sell offers, leading to increased conversion rates.

Final Thoughts

Executive sponsorship and buy-in are integral to driving customer success within enterprise companies. By taking steps to establish leadership and KPI alignment, executive education, and clear communication channels, organizations can secure the active support of senior executives in customer success initiatives.

Measuring metrics like customer satisfaction, customer retention rate, and upsell/cross-sell revenue provides insights into the degree and effectiveness of executive sponsorship. Real-world examples from companies like Amazon, Salesforce, and Adobe highlight the impact of executive sponsorship.

Ultimately, executive sponsorship and buy-in demonstrate a strong commitment to customer success, drive customer retention, and enhance upselling and cross-selling efforts. Leveraging executive support empowers enterprise companies to foster a customer-centric culture, improve customer relationships, and achieve long-term success.

Chapter Forty-Five
Harnessing Company Culture and Values

In this chapter, we will explore the importance of company culture and values in driving customer success for enterprise companies. We will discuss techniques to implement a strong and customer-centric culture, metrics to measure the impact of culture on customer success, real-world examples of companies that have successfully leveraged their culture to retain customers, and how this strategy can improve upsell and cross-sell opportunities.

By aligning the organization's culture and values with customer success goals, companies can create an environment that fosters customer-centricity, employee engagement, and long-term business growth.

Why Company Culture and Values Matter

In enterprise companies, where complexity, scale, and sophistication are crucial, the significance of company culture and values in driving customer success cannot be overstated. While robust products and cutting-edge solutions play a vital role, intangible elements like culture and values form the bedrock of exceptional customer relationships and long-term success.

A customer-centric culture isn't born overnight; it's cultivated through deliberate effort and a shared commitment to delivering value beyond expectations. At its core, this culture places the customer at the heart of every decision, interaction, and process. In enterprise companies, where numerous departments collaborate to serve customers, a unified culture ensures seamless coordination and consistent customer experiences. When every employee, from the C-suite to frontline staff, shares a common understanding of putting the customer first, an environment of trust, loyalty, and mutual growth is fostered.

Values serve as guiding principles that shape behaviors, decisions, and interactions within an organization. When these values are closely aligned with customer success objectives, a powerful synergy emerges. For instance, integrity becomes critical to building trust with customers, innovation drives the creation of tailored solutions, and collaboration ensures seamless cross-functional support. When values resonate with both employees and customers, an authentic connection is born that extends beyond transactions, nurturing enduring partnerships built on shared principles.

A company culture that values customer success elevates employee engagement and empowerment. When employees understand the impact of their contributions on customers and witness the organization's commitment to customer well-being, they derive a sense of purpose from their work. This intrinsic motivation fuels proactive problem-solving, a dedication to continuous improvement, and a willingness to go the extra mile for customers. A culture that prioritizes customer success becomes a catalyst for employee growth and satisfaction.

Company culture isn't static; it evolves in response to changing customer needs, market dynamics, and industry trends. Customer insights play a pivotal role in this evolution. Regularly collecting and analyzing feedback helps enterprise companies align their culture with the evolving expectations of their customers. As customer success teams uncover pain points, desires, and emerging opportunities, they inform the company's cultural evolution, leading to more relevant strategies and solutions.

In an enterprise setting, customer interactions span multiple touchpoints, from sales and onboarding to support and account management. A well-defined culture and set of values ensure that customer success principles permeate each of these touchpoints. This consistency reinforces the customer's perception of a holistic and dedicated partnership. Whether a customer interacts with a sales representative, a technical support agent, or a product specialist, the culture and values should resonate, creating a seamless and satisfying experience.

A culture that champions customer success instills a sense of accountability and responsibility throughout the organization. Teams recognize that their performance directly impacts the customer's success, creating a culture of ownership. Individuals take pride in their contributions, hold themselves to high standards, and seek out opportunities to exceed customer expectations. This culture of accountability not only improves customer relationships but also enhances internal collaboration and efficiency.

Best Practices for Establishing a Strong Company Culture

- *Define core values:* Clearly define and communicate the core values that drive the organization's mission and vision for customer success.

- *Lead by example:* Ensure that leaders embody the company's values and consistently demonstrate customer-centric behavior.

- *Hire for cultural fit:* During the hiring process, prioritize candidates who align with the company's values and can contribute to a positive and customer-focused culture.

- *Training and development:* Provide ongoing training and development opportunities that reinforce the organization's values and equip employees with the skills needed to deliver exceptional customer success.

- *Recognition and rewards:* Establish recognition programs that celebrate employees who embody the company's values and consistently deliver outstanding customer experiences.

Metrics to Measure

- *Employee satisfaction and engagement:* Measure employee satisfaction and engagement levels to gauge the effectiveness of the company culture in driving motivation and commitment.

- *Customer satisfaction and retention:* Track CSAT scores and retention rates to assess the impact of the company culture on customer loyalty and long-term relationships.
- *Employee advocacy:* Monitor employee advocacy metrics, such as referrals and positive reviews, to measure the extent to which employees align with and promote the company's values.
- *Employee retention:* Measure employee turnover rates to gauge the success of the company culture in fostering a supportive and engaging work environment.

Real-World Examples

- *Zappos:* The online shoe and clothing retailer Zappos is renowned for its strong company culture and commitment to delivering exceptional customer service. The company's emphasis on core values like "Deliver WOW through service" has contributed to its success in retaining customers and driving business growth.
- *Patagonia:* Outdoor retailer Patagonia's commitment to environmental sustainability is deeply ingrained in the company culture. By aligning company values with customer values, Patagonia has fostered a loyal customer base and achieved strong brand loyalty.

Why Company Culture and Values Aid Customer Retention

A strong company culture and values system creates a cohesive and customer-centric organization. When employees are aligned with the company's mission, values, and commitment to customer success, they are more motivated, engaged, and empowered to deliver exceptional experiences. This leads to higher customer satisfaction, increased trust, and, ultimately, customer loyalty and retention.

How Building a Strong Company Culture and Values Can Improve Upsell and Cross-Sell Opportunities

A customer-centric culture and values system provides a solid foundation for upsell and cross-sell opportunities. When employees understand and embody the company's values, they are better equipped to identify additional value propositions and recommend relevant products or services to customers. This, in turn, increases customer lifetime value and drives revenue growth through upselling and cross-selling initiatives.

Final Thoughts

Company culture and values play a crucial role in driving customer success for enterprise companies.

For success, you will need to prioritize training and development, ensure executives lead by example, and hire new employees based on their cultural fit. You can draw inspiration from real-world examples like Patagonia and Zappos to create a positive work environment that fosters customer loyalty, employee engagement, and business growth.

By aligning company culture with customer success objectives, enterprise companies can build strong, long-term relationships with their customers and maximize upsell.

Chapter Forty-Six
Boosting Employee Engagement and Satisfaction

Client success is not solely dependent on product features or pricing. The engagement and satisfaction of employees play a crucial role in delivering exceptional customer experiences and driving long-term customer success.

This chapter explores the significance of employee engagement and satisfaction in enterprise companies' customer success strategies. We'll look at how having happy employees could make all the difference to your customer retention and upsell and cross-sell efforts.

Why Employee Engagement and Satisfaction Matter

Customer success strategies often focus on meeting customer needs and expectations, but an integral yet often underestimated aspect of these strategies is the engagement and satisfaction of employees.

Employee engagement goes beyond mere job satisfaction. It embodies the emotional commitment and dedication that employees have toward their roles and the organization as a whole. In the context of customer success, engaged employees display a higher degree of empathy, accountability, and ownership. They are intrinsically motivated to go the extra mile for customers, seeking innovative solutions and demonstrating a genuine concern for customer well-being. This level of engagement is a linchpin in creating memorable customer experiences that foster trust, loyalty, and advocacy.

Engaged employees are empowered employees. Enterprise companies that prioritize employee engagement grant their customer success teams the autonomy to make informed decisions and tailor solutions. This empowerment fuels a sense of responsibility and ownership over customer outcomes. This is particularly critical in the enterprise realm, where customers often require intricate and customized solutions. Empowered employees are more likely to devise creative approaches and navigate complex challenges, enhancing the overall customer experience.

Employee satisfaction forms the bedrock upon which engagement flourishes. It encompasses factors such as work–life balance, career growth opportunities, a positive work environment, and recognition. When employees feel valued and supported, their dedication to their roles and the organization deepens. In the context of enterprise customer success, where relationships can span years, satisfied employees are more likely to stay committed, fostering the consistent service quality that customers rely upon.

Enterprise customer relationships are multifaceted, involving a network of stakeholders across both organizations. Engaged and satisfied customer success teams act as ambassadors, representing the company's dedication to service excellence. Customers recognize the passion and commitment these teams bring to the table, establishing a foundation of trust and reliability. The rapport built by engaged and satisfied employees extends beyond transactions, evolving into long-term partnerships grounded in mutual respect and shared goals.

Engaged employees also possess an inherent curiosity and dedication to continuous learning — invaluable traits when dealing with multifaceted customer needs. Their eagerness to collaborate, understand customer pain points, and offer innovative solutions elevates the customer experience and positions the enterprise company as a true partner in the customer's journey.

The Impact of High Employee Turnover

Employee turnover in the customer success domain can disrupt customer relationships, leading to inconsistency and a lack of familiarity. Engaged and satisfied employees are more likely to stay with the organization, providing a stable foundation for customer relationships. This retention of talent ensures that customer success teams have institutional knowledge, understand customer nuances, and can anticipate evolving needs, thus delivering a seamless and consistent experience.

Best Practices for Ensuring Employee Engagement and Satisfaction

- *Foster a positive work environment:* Create a workplace culture that values collaboration, open communication, and mutual respect. Encourage teamwork, provide opportunities for professional growth, and ensure employees feel supported and appreciated.
- *Empower employees:* Delegate decision-making authority, encourage autonomy, and provide opportunities for

employees to take ownership of their work. Empowered employees are more likely to be proactive, innovative, and invested in delivering exceptional customer experiences.

- *Provide ongoing training and development:* Invest in employee skill development, provide relevant training programs, and encourage continuous learning. Equipping employees with the necessary knowledge and tools enhances their confidence and ability to meet customer needs effectively.

- *Recognize and reward achievements:* Implement a robust recognition and rewards program that acknowledges and celebrates employee contributions. Recognizing exceptional performance and providing incentives not only boosts morale but also reinforces the importance of delivering outstanding customer experiences. (More on incentives and bonuses in Chapter 41.)

Metrics to Measure

- *Employee satisfaction and engagement:* Conduct regular employee satisfaction surveys to gauge overall job satisfaction, motivation, and commitment. Measure engagement levels to understand the degree of emotional connection employees have with their work and the organization.

- *Employee retention:* Monitor employee turnover rates to assess the effectiveness of your employee engagement strategies. A low turnover rate indicates that employees are satisfied and motivated to stay, leading to better customer relationships.

- *Customer satisfaction and retention:* Track CSAT scores and retention rates to evaluate the impact of employee engagement on customer success. Satisfied and engaged employees are more likely to deliver exceptional customer experiences, leading to higher customer satisfaction and loyalty.

Real-World Examples

- *Google:* Google is renowned for its employee-centric culture. The company offers a range of perks, including flexible work hours, onsite amenities, and career development opportunities. Prioritizing employee engagement and satisfaction has enabled Google to build a strong foundation for delivering innovative products and outstanding customer experiences.
- *Southwest Airlines:* Southwest Airlines places a strong emphasis on employee engagement and satisfaction, recognizing the direct link between employee happiness and customer loyalty. By nurturing a supportive and positive work environment, Southwest Airlines consistently delivers exceptional service and retains a loyal customer base.

Why Employee Engagement and Satisfaction Aid Customer Retention

Employee engagement and satisfaction directly impact customer experiences and ultimately influence customer retention.

Engaged and satisfied employees are more likely to go above and beyond to meet customer needs, exhibit higher levels of empathy, and build stronger relationships. These positive interactions create a sense of trust and loyalty, leading to increased customer retention rates.

How Employee Engagement and Satisfaction Can Improve Upsell and Cross-Sell Opportunities

Satisfied and engaged employees possess a deep understanding of customer preferences, pain points, and needs. By fostering a culture of continuous learning and empowerment, employees can identify upsell and cross-sell opportunities more effectively. Their expertise and knowledge enable them to provide personalized recommendations and tailor offerings to customer requirements, leading to increased revenue and customer lifetime value.

Final Thoughts

Taking steps to improve employee engagement and satisfaction is a powerful approach for enterprise companies wanting to drive customer success.

By following best practices to foster a positive work environment, measuring key metrics, and drawing insights from real-world examples, organizations can create a culture that empowers employees to deliver exceptional customer experiences. This, in turn, leads to higher customer retention rates, increased upsell and cross-sell opportunities, and sustained business growth.

Embracing employee engagement and satisfaction is not just beneficial for the workforce but also a key driver of customer success in today's competitive business landscape.

Part IX: Leadership and Future Planning

"The faster you can help customers understand and extract value from your product that is in line with their business goals the stickier and more successful they'll be."

— Jeff Gardner, President and CEO, Brings Home Security

Chapter Forty-Seven

Training and Development Opportunities for CSMs

Training and development opportunities are crucial for the success of customer success teams in enterprise companies. This chapter explores the significance of investing in continuous learning and growth for employees, best practices for implementing effective training programs, the metrics you can monitor to measure their impact, real-world examples from leading companies, and the positive effects you can expect to see on customer retention, upsells, and cross-sells.

What Are Training and Development Opportunities?

In a highly effective and successful customer success department, there are various training opportunities available to customer success managers (CSMs) to enhance their skills and expertise. Some of these training opportunities include:

- *Product training:* CSMs should receive comprehensive product training to ensure they have a deep understanding of the company's offerings. This training covers the product's features, use cases, and benefits, enabling CSMs to effectively communicate its value to customers and help them optimize its usage.

- *Customer success methodologies:* Training on customer success methodologies provides CSMs with frameworks and best practices for managing customer relationships, driving adoption, and achieving positive customer outcomes. This training equips them with the tools they need to create personalized success plans for each customer.

- *Communication and relationship building:* Effective communication is crucial for CSMs to build strong relationships with customers. Training in communication skills, active listening, and empathy helps CSMs to understand customer needs, address concerns, and proactively engage with customers.

- *Problem-solving and conflict resolution:* CSMs should be trained in problem-solving techniques and conflict resolution strategies so that they can handle challenging customer situations effectively. This training enables them to navigate difficult conversations and find constructive solutions.

- *Time management and prioritization:* Training in time management and prioritization equips CSMs with the skills they need to manage their workload efficiently. This ensures that they can dedicate ample time and attention to each customer, fostering personalized support.

- *Customer data analysis:* Training in data analysis allows CSMs to interpret customer data, track key performance metrics, and identify trends and patterns in customer behavior. This analytical skillset helps them proactively address customer needs and opportunities.

- *Upselling and cross-selling:* CSMs can receive training in upselling and cross-selling techniques to identify expansion opportunities within existing accounts. This training helps them uncover additional value for customers and drive revenue growth.

- *Industry knowledge:* CSMs should undergo continuous training to stay up to date with industry trends, best practices, and market developments. This knowledge enables them to provide relevant insights and guidance to customers in their specific industries.

- *Customer service excellence:* Training in customer service excellence ensures that CSMs are equipped to consistently deliver exceptional customer experiences. This training emphasizes the importance of customer-centricity and a proactive approach to customer support.

- *Personal development:* CSMs should have access to personal development training on topics such as leadership skills, emotional intelligence, and career growth. This training fosters a growth mindset and helps CSMs to continuously improve their performance.

In a successful customer success department, these training opportunities are provided regularly and supported by a culture of continuous learning.

Best Practices for Training and Development

- *Assess needs:* Conduct a thorough assessment of the skills and knowledge gaps within the customer success team to identify specific training needs.

- *Create a comprehensive training program:* Develop a well-structured training program that encompasses the technical and soft skills required for effective customer success.

- *Blend learning approaches:* Use a mix of training methods, including instructor-led sessions, e-learning modules, on-the-job training, workshops, and mentorship programs. This will enable you to cater to diverse learning styles.

- *Foster continuous learning:* Encourage a culture of continuous learning and development by providing access to online resources, industry conferences, and professional certifications.

- *Encourage collaboration:* Facilitate knowledge sharing and collaboration among team members through regular team meetings, cross-functional projects, and peer mentoring.

Metrics to Measure

- *Training completion rates:* Measure the percentage of employees who have successfully completed the training programs on offer.

- *Skill development assessment:* Assess the improvement in specific skills and knowledge areas before and after training to gauge the effectiveness of the programs.

- *Customer satisfaction (CSAT) and retention:* Monitor (CSAT) scores and retention rates to identify any positive correlation with the implementation of training initiatives.

- *Upsell and cross-sell revenue:* Track the impact of training programs on the success of upselling and cross-selling efforts by monitoring revenue generated from these activities.

Real-World Examples

The following real-world examples illustrate how leading companies recognize the importance of CSM training and development. By providing their CSMs with a wide range of training opportunities and fostering a culture of continuous learning, they not only enhance their team's capabilities but also achieve higher customer satisfaction, retention rates, and revenue growth through effective customer success strategies.

Microsoft

Technology giant Microsoft invests significantly in training and development opportunities for its customer success teams. The company provides CSMs with comprehensive training on its diverse product offerings, ensuring they are well-equipped to guide customers in optimizing their use of Microsoft's solutions.

Moreover, Microsoft focuses on enhancing CSMs' communication and problem-solving skills, empowering them to address complex customer needs and build strong relationships.

The company also encourages continuous learning through access to industry-specific knowledge and trends, fostering expertise among CSMs. This investment in training has contributed to Microsoft's ability to deliver exceptional customer experiences and drive customer loyalty, leading to sustained growth and success in a competitive industry.

Amazon Web Services (AWS)

AWS, a global leader in cloud computing services, places a strong emphasis on training and development for its customer success managers. The company offers extensive product training to ensure CSMs have a deep understanding of AWS cloud solutions. This includes hands-on labs, virtual classrooms, and access to a vast array of online resources.

AWS also provides ongoing training in customer success methodologies, enabling CSMs to effectively manage client relationships, drive adoption, and create customized success strategies. The brand's commitment to continuous learning has resulted in a highly skilled customer success team capable of helping clients optimize their cloud infrastructure.

Overall, this focus on training has led to increased customer satisfaction, loyalty, and business growth.

Why Training and Development for CSMs Aids Customer Retention

Training equips customer success managers with the skills and knowledge necessary to address customer needs effectively, thereby improving customer satisfaction and loyalty.

It also aids problem-solving, seeing how well-trained customer success managers can anticipate and address customer issues proactively, minimizing the risk of churn.

Training also enables personalized engagement. Training programs empower customer success teams to provide personalized support, tailor recommendations, and uncover upsell and cross-sell opportunities based on a deep understanding of each customer's unique requirements.

How This Strategy Can Improve Upsell and Cross-Sell Opportunities

Training enhances a CSM's understanding of the product or service your company offers, enabling them to identify upsell and cross-sell opportunities and effectively communicate their value to customers.

It also enables a consultative approach. Well-trained CSMs can act as trusted advisors, guiding customers through their journeys, understanding their evolving needs, and presenting relevant upsell and cross-sell options when appropriate.

Final Thoughts

The significance of training and development opportunities for customer success teams in enterprise companies cannot be overstated. These programs serve as the cornerstone of a successful customer-centric approach, with the potential to deliver remarkable results.

By providing comprehensive training opportunities to customer success managers, organizations equip their teams with the skills and knowledge necessary to excel. This, in turn, has a profound impact on customer retention and satisfaction, as well as the ability to maximize upselling and cross-selling opportunities.

Training empowers CSMs to become product experts, enabling them to effectively communicate the value of offerings to customers and help them optimize their usage. Moreover, it equips CSMs with the tools and frameworks needed to foster strong customer relationships, drive adoption, and achieve customer outcomes. Effective communication, problem-solving, and time management skills cultivated through training enable CSMs to better understand and address customer needs, ultimately enhancing the overall customer experience.

Furthermore, training programs instill a culture of continuous learning, ensuring that CSMs stay updated with industry trends, best practices, and market developments. This industry knowledge enables CSMs to share relevant insights and guidance with customers in their specific domains, reinforcing their position as trusted advisors.

In essence, when you implement training and development for CSMs, you are investing in the future of customer success. CSMs are empowered to understand and effectively cater to customer needs, fostering loyalty and reducing churn. Moreover, well-trained CSMs can identify upsell and cross-sell opportunities and guide customers through their journeys because they are considered trusted advisors.

As organizations continue to prioritize training and development, they position themselves as partners in their customers' success stories. By enhancing employee skills and knowledge, they ultimately enhance customer satisfaction, retention, and revenue, solidifying their place as leaders in the ever-evolving landscape of customer success.

Chapter Forty-Eight
Leadership and Management Development

Effective leadership and management are crucial for customer success teams in enterprise companies. By investing in developing strong leaders and managers, organizations can foster a culture of excellence, drive team performance, and achieve sustainable business growth.

Let's look at this in more detail.

Why Leadership and Management Development Matter

Customer success has transitioned from a transactional service to a strategic imperative for businesses. With increasing competition and the rise of customer-centric cultures, organizations must now go beyond mere customer satisfaction to build lasting relationships and secure customer loyalty. This paradigm shift has spotlighted the role of leadership and management in orchestrating customer success initiatives.

Leadership in the context of customer success is not just about overseeing tasks; it involves inspiring and guiding teams to deliver unparalleled value to customers. Effective leaders set the tone for the entire team, instilling a sense of purpose and fostering a customer-first mindset. They empower their teams to proactively address customer needs, navigate challenges, and create innovative solutions.

Leadership development equips individuals with the skills to communicate effectively, motivate their teams, and align everyone toward a shared vision of exceptional customer experiences.

While leadership sets the direction, management ensures the efficient execution of customer success strategies. Effective management is the backbone of operational excellence, enabling teams to deliver consistent and high-quality services. Skillful management ensures resource allocation, process optimization, and timely responses to customer inquiries, all of which contribute to building trust and satisfaction. Development in management skills enables individuals to streamline operations, manage workload, and maintain a well-coordinated customer success framework.

Leadership and management development in customer success also nurtures the art of strategic decision-making and adaptability. Customer needs are dynamic and can evolve rapidly due to market shifts or technological advancements. Leaders equipped with strategic thinking skills can anticipate these changes and proactively realign their customer success strategies. Adaptive leadership and management practices ensure that teams can swiftly pivot to meet new challenges, seize emerging opportunities, and stay ahead of industry trends.

A strong leadership and management framework fosters a culture of continuous improvement. When leaders and managers prioritize growth and development, they set a precedent for their teams to do the same. This culture trickles down to every aspect of customer success, from refining communication approaches to enhancing problem-solving techniques. A commitment to improvement becomes a driving force, enabling customer success teams to exceed expectations and consistently drive customer loyalty.

Investing in leadership and management development within customer success has a ripple effect on employee engagement and retention. (More on this in Chapter 46.) Skilled leaders and managers create an environment of trust and support, motivating team members to invest in their roles. This engagement not only boosts productivity but also contributes to employee satisfaction and longevity. Well-developed leaders and managers provide career growth opportunities and mentorship, leading to a more committed and motivated workforce.

The significance of leadership and management development in customer success cannot be ignored in today's competitive business landscape. Effective leadership drives team dynamics, shapes organizational culture, and propels customer success strategies, while efficient management ensures operational excellence and adaptability. The symbiotic relationship between leadership, management, and customer success contributes to enduring customer relationships, sustained growth, and a distinctive competitive edge. Organizations that prioritize and invest in the development of their customer success leaders position themselves for long-term success in the ever-evolving realm of customer satisfaction.

Leadership and Management Development Best Practices

- *Leadership development programs:* Implement structured leadership development programs that focus on enhancing leadership skills, strategic thinking, decision-making, and fostering a customer-centric mindset.

- *Mentoring and coaching:* Provide mentoring and coaching opportunities to support the growth and development of leaders and managers, fostering their ability to inspire, motivate, and guide their teams.

- *Performance management:* Implement performance management systems that provide regular feedback, goal-setting, and performance evaluation to drive continuous improvement and accountability in customer success leadership.

- *Communication and collaboration:* Foster a culture of open communication and collaboration, encouraging leaders and managers to actively engage with their teams, share knowledge, and facilitate cross-functional collaboration.

Metrics to Measure

- *Leadership effectiveness:* Assess leadership effectiveness through feedback surveys, 360-degree evaluations, and performance reviews to gauge the impact of leadership development initiatives on team performance and customer satisfaction.

- *Employee engagement:* Measure employee engagement levels through surveys, assessing factors such as job satisfaction, motivation, and commitment to evaluate the effectiveness of leadership and management practices in driving employee satisfaction.

- *Customer retention:* Track customer retention rates to determine the influence of strong leadership and management on customer loyalty and long-term relationships.
- *Upsell and cross-sell revenue:* Measure the impact of leadership and management development on upselling and cross-selling efforts by monitoring the revenue generated from existing customers and identifying opportunities for expansion.

Real-World Example

HubSpot

HubSpot, a leading inbound marketing and sales platform, prioritizes leadership and management development in its customer success teams. The company recognizes that effective leadership sets the tone for the entire organization, especially in customer-facing roles. As such, HubSpot provides mentoring and coaching opportunities to support the growth and development of its leaders and managers.

As a result of these efforts, HubSpot has achieved remarkable levels of employee engagement. Team members in customer success roles report high job satisfaction, motivation, and commitment to their work. This engagement directly translates into improved customer experiences and higher customer retention rates. HubSpot's leaders and managers, who have benefited from ongoing development, create an environment of trust and support that motivates team members to excel in their roles. This, in turn, contributes to HubSpot's impressive customer success and sustained growth in the competitive marketing technology industry.

This example underscores the critical role that leadership and management development play in enhancing customer success, driving customer satisfaction, and ensuring sustainable business growth. HubSpot has leveraged these practices to not only retain customers but thrive in highly competitive markets.

Why Leadership and Management Development Aid Customer Retention

Investing in leadership and management development contributes to customer retention by fostering strong team leadership, effective communication, and a customer-centric culture. Well-trained leaders and managers can effectively guide their teams to resolve customer issues and proactively address their needs, resulting in enhanced customer satisfaction and loyalty.

How Leadership and Management Development Can Improve Upsell and Cross-sell Opportunities

Leadership and management development enable customer success teams to develop a strategic and consultative approach to customer engagement. Effective leaders can identify upsell and cross-sell opportunities, leverage customer insights, and align their team's efforts to maximize revenue potential.

Final Thoughts

Effective leadership and management are pivotal in the success of customer success teams within enterprise organizations. Investing in the development of strong leaders and managers fosters a culture of excellence, enhances team performance, and fuels sustainable business growth. The shift of customer success from a transactional service to a strategic imperative necessitates skilled leadership and management to orchestrate these initiatives effectively.

Leadership in customer success is not just about overseeing tasks; it involves inspiring and guiding teams to deliver exceptional value to customers. Leaders set the tone, instill a customer-first mindset, and empower teams to proactively address customer needs. Management ensures the efficient execution of customer success strategies, fostering operational excellence and trust. These leaders also cultivate strategic thinking and adaptability, enabling teams to pivot swiftly in response to evolving customer needs.

A culture of continuous improvement emerges from leadership and management development. It trickles into every facet of customer success, from refining communication approaches to enhancing problem-solving techniques. This commitment to growth has a ripple effect, boosting employee engagement and retention. Well-developed leaders and managers create an environment of trust and support, motivating team members to excel in their roles.

In today's competitive landscape, it's imperative to prioritize development for leaders and managers in customer success departments. They shape organizational culture, drive strategies, and ensure operational excellence. This synergy between leadership, management, and customer success establishes enduring customer relationships, sustains growth, and provides a distinct competitive edge.

Chapter Forty-Nine
Succession Planning for Customer Success Teams

Succession planning, a proactive and methodical approach, emerges as a pivotal strategy to ensure the seamless transition of leadership roles while maintaining the organization's commitment to delivering exceptional customer experiences.

Succession planning involves identifying and developing future leaders within an organization. By strategically grooming internal talent, companies can ensure continuity, maintain high levels of customer satisfaction, and drive long-term success.

We will discuss techniques to implement succession planning, metrics to measure its effectiveness, real-world examples from leading companies, and explore how this strategy can improve upsell and cross-sell opportunities. By embracing succession planning, customer success teams can build a strong foundation for sustained growth and customer retention.

Understanding Succession Planning

Succession planning is a comprehensive strategy that involves identifying, developing, and preparing individuals within an organization to assume key leadership roles in the future. This approach aims to mitigate the potential risks associated with sudden leadership vacuums and align the organization's long-term objectives with the talents and capabilities of its upcoming leaders.

Customer success leaders hold a distinctive role within an organization, as they are tasked with building and maintaining strong relationships with customers, ensuring their satisfaction and continued loyalty. These leaders are entrusted with the responsibility of understanding customer needs, addressing concerns, and driving business growth through customer retention and expansion. Consequently, the selection and development of future customer success leaders must be approached with careful consideration.

One of the fundamental pillars of succession planning is the proactive identification of potential leaders. This involves recognizing individuals within the organization who exhibit a combination of skills, attributes, and values aligned with the customer success leadership role. These traits might include exceptional communication skills, empathy, strategic thinking, and a passion for customer satisfaction. By identifying such individuals early on, organizations can embark on tailored developmental journeys that prepare them to excel in future leadership positions.

Once potential customer success leaders have been identified, organizations should invest in comprehensive training programs designed to enhance their leadership skills, industry knowledge, and understanding of customer needs. These programs can encompass mentorship, leadership workshops, cross-functional exposure, and access to resources that broaden the employee's perspective on customer success management.

At the heart of effective succession planning lies the cultivation of a culture that values continuous learning and growth. Organizations must foster an environment where aspiring leaders feel empowered to take ownership of their development, seek out challenges, and embrace new experiences. This culture encourages individuals to step outside of their comfort zones and acquire the diverse skills necessary for customer success leadership.

Mentorship also plays a pivotal role in succession planning, allowing current customer success leaders to impart their wisdom and experiences to their successors. This knowledge transfer not only helps aspiring leaders gain valuable insights but also ensures the preservation of organizational values and best practices. Mentorship provides a platform for candid discussions, feedback, and guidance, fostering a strong bond between current and future leaders.

In an era characterized by technological advancements and shifting customer expectations, succession planning must adapt to the evolving landscapes. This requires a keen awareness of emerging trends, digital tools, and innovative strategies that shape customer success dynamics. Organizations should incorporate agility into their succession planning efforts, equipping future leaders with the skills to navigate these changes while upholding the core principles of customer satisfaction.

Succession Planning Best Practices

- *Identify high-potential employees:* Implement a talent identification process to identify individuals with the potential to assume leadership roles in the future. Assess their skills, competencies, and alignment with the organization's values and customer-centric ethos.

- *Develop a leadership development program:* Create a structured program that provides aspiring leaders with the necessary training, mentoring, and exposure to different aspects of the business. Offer opportunities for skill development, such as leadership workshops, cross-functional projects, and external learning experiences.

- *Establish a succession planning committee:* Form a dedicated committee responsible for overseeing the succession planning process. This committee should include representatives from various departments to ensure a holistic and unbiased approach.

- *Conduct regular performance reviews:* Continuously evaluate the performance and potential of employees. Provide constructive feedback, identify areas for development, and create personalized development plans to nurture their growth.

- *Encourage knowledge sharing and mentorship:* Foster a culture of knowledge sharing and mentorship within the organization. Encourage experienced leaders to mentor and guide emerging talent, transferring valuable insights and industry expertise.

Metrics to Measure

- *Succession pipeline:* Measure the number of high-potential employees in the succession pipeline and track their progress over time.

- *Internal promotions:* Monitor the percentage of leadership positions filled internally through succession planning efforts.

- *Employee satisfaction and engagement:* Assess employee satisfaction and engagement levels. A high level of engagement often indicates the effectiveness of succession planning in fostering career growth and development opportunities.

- *Employee retention:* Measure the retention rate of high-potential employees and evaluate whether they stay with the organization as they progress in their careers.
- *Successor performance:* Evaluate the performance of individuals who have been promoted through the succession planning process to assess their effectiveness in their new roles.

Real-World Examples

- *Google:* Google's "Emerging Leaders Program" identifies high-potential employees and provides them with a customized development plan, including training, mentorship, and stretch assignments. This program has helped Google nurture future leaders and maintain a talent pipeline for critical roles.
- *Salesforce:* Salesforce implements a mentorship program called "Futureforce," which pairs high-potential employees with experienced leaders. This initiative enables knowledge transfer, skill development, and preparation for future leadership roles.

Why Succession Planning Aids Customer Retention

Succession planning ensures a smooth transition of leadership within customer success teams, minimizing disruptions and maintaining consistent service delivery to customers.

Successors who have been groomed within the organization are more likely to have a deep understanding of customer needs and preferences, allowing for a seamless continuation of customer relationships.

Succession planning also helps preserve institutional knowledge within the organization. The retained knowledge contributes to better customer support and a higher level of customer satisfaction.

How Succession Planning Improves Upsell and Cross-Sell Opportunities

Succession planning plays a vital role in ensuring that customer relationships smoothly transition to new leaders, minimizing the chances of any disruptions and facilitating a seamless process for upselling and cross-selling.

When customers have built a solid connection with their designated customer success manager, the shift to a new manager becomes a smoother experience. This enables an uninterrupted focus on recognizing potential upsell and cross-sell prospects, as the customer's comfort with the transition allows the business relationship to flourish.

Succession planning plays a key role in knowledge sharing as it facilitates the transfer of wisdom and know-how from seasoned CSMs to their successors. This passing of knowledge empowers successors with a comprehensive grasp of customer requirements, challenges, and avenues for expansion. This enriched understanding positions them well to recognize and present opportunities for upselling and cross-selling, as they are armed with valuable insights.

Having a plan in place for seamless transitions through succession planning also brings about proactive account management. This means that whenever a CSM transitions to a new role, there's already a designated successor prepared to step in. This proactive approach guarantees uninterrupted support for customers and empowers the successor to quickly spot potential upsell and cross-sell prospects, leading to increased revenue growth.

Final Thoughts

Succession planning plays a vital role in the long-term success of customer success teams in enterprise companies. By proactively identifying and developing internal talent, organizations can ensure a smooth leadership transition, maintain customer continuity, and drive customer satisfaction.

Succession planning also provides opportunities for employee growth and development, leading to higher engagement and retention rates. Leveraging succession planning allows future customer success leaders to foster strong relationships with customers, hit the ground running when it comes to upselling and cross-selling, and contribute to the organization's overall growth and profitability.

Embracing succession planning is a proactive step toward building a robust and resilient customer success function equipped to meet the evolving needs of customers in the dynamic business landscape.

Chapter Fifty
Conclusion: Embracing a Customer Success Mindset

In this final chapter of *Customer Success Mastery*, we explore the transformative power of embracing a customer success mindset and adopting a retention strategy across all aspects of business.

Throughout this book, we have delved into the fundamental principles of customer success, examining how it extends beyond a mere department or strategy. Instead, it is an organizational culture that fuels sustainable growth and fosters meaningful relationships with customers.

By prioritizing customer success, organizations have the unique opportunity to create genuine connections with their customers, understanding their needs, challenges, and aspirations. We have seen how this mindset empowers businesses to proactively anticipate customer requirements, tailor solutions to meet their specific demands, and guide them toward their desired outcomes.

Moreover, the journey to embracing a customer success mindset requires unwavering commitment from leadership and cohesive collaboration between all departments. This book has emphasized the significance of executive sponsorship, aligning company goals, and investing in comprehensive training programs to equip every member of the customer success team with the skills and knowledge needed to excel.

As we conclude this transformative journey, it is evident that the path to a customer success mindset is not without challenges. The rewards, however, are immeasurable. Companies that embrace this mindset will not only find themselves achieving remarkable customer retention and loyalty but also driving increased revenue, profitability, and overall success.

In a world where customer expectations are ever-evolving, embracing a customer success mindset becomes a differentiating factor, setting exceptional organizations apart from the rest. This book serves as a guiding light for those seeking to embark on this transformative journey, and it is my hope that the insights shared here will inspire and empower leaders, teams, and individuals to cultivate a customer-centric culture that transcends the boundaries of time and industry.

As we close this book, let us remember that customer success is not a destination but an ever-evolving philosophy that propels us forward on a journey of continuous improvement, empathy, and relentless dedication to the success and satisfaction of our valued customers. Embrace the customer success mindset, and together, let us forge a future where every interaction with our customers becomes a remarkable testament to the power of putting their success at the heart of all that we do.

Final Thoughts From the Author

Dear Reader,

As we come to the end of this book, I want to take a moment to express my deepest gratitude for joining me on this journey through 50 powerful techniques and strategies for your customer success department. It has been an honor to share my expertise with you, and I sincerely hope that the insights and ideas presented throughout these pages have been valuable to you and your organization.

In today's competitive business landscape, customer success has emerged as a critical differentiator for enterprises. The ability to build strong, long-lasting relationships with customers and drive their success is critical to sustainable growth and profitability. By investing in a robust customer success strategy and implementing the techniques and strategies outlined in this book, you are taking a significant step toward achieving your organizational goals.

Throughout this book, we have explored a wide range of topics, from leveraging technology and data to nurturing customer relationships, optimizing processes, and fostering a culture of success. Each chapter has provided practical advice, real-world examples, and actionable steps to help you enhance your customer success efforts and deliver exceptional value to your customers.

I hope that you have found inspiration in the stories of successful companies that have implemented these strategies to drive their customer success initiatives. From industry giants like Salesforce, Amazon Web Services, and HubSpot to innovative startups, these organizations have demonstrated the transformative power of customer success when executed effectively.

As you embark on implementing these techniques and strategies within your own customer success department, remember that success is a journey, not a destination. It requires dedication, perseverance, and an unwavering commitment to continuous improvement. Embrace a mindset of learning and innovation, and be open to adapting your approach based on the evolving needs and preferences of your customers.

Finally, I want to express my sincere appreciation for your trust in me as your guide through this exploration of customer success. I hope that the knowledge and insights you have gained from this book will empower you to build a world-class customer success department that exceeds expectations, drives customer satisfaction, and fuels long-term business growth.

Thank you once again for joining me on this enlightening journey. May your customer success endeavors be filled with remarkable achievements and meaningful connections with your customers.

Jeffrey Ray Rogers
VP of Customer Success and Global Support

ABOUT THE AUTHOR

Jeffrey Rogers is a seasoned expert at the intersection of finance, information security, and customer success. With a bachelor's degree in finance from the University of Kentucky and a master's degree in information assurance from Capital Technical University, he brings a unique blend of financial acumen and cybersecurity knowledge to his work.

His passion for knowledge extends beyond the classroom and boardroom. Having traveled to over 54 countries, Jeffrey embraces diverse cultures and experiences, sharing these worldly perspectives with his family of five. He finds immense happiness in exploring the globe alongside his loved ones.

As a proven leader in customer success departments, his career has seen him build and lead successful customer success teams in three tech startups, resulting in triumphant exits and securing capital investments at Series B and C levels. His dedication to maximizing customer lifetime value, developing growth strategies, and ensuring a positive customer experience has been instrumental to his success.

Since 2006, Jeffrey has lent his expertise as a consultant in the fields of customer success, customer experience, customer loyalty, and customer success design. He partners with businesses to craft exceptional customer experiences through customer-centric strategies, feedback systems, and comprehensive training programs.

Jeffrey has graced prestigious stages, including RSA, ISACs, SaaS leadership conventions, PhishMe's annual Submerge event, Gainsight's Pulse conferences, and tech summits. His engaging presentations are tailored to meet the specific needs of his audience, aiming to inspire and educate on the art of improving customer experiences and driving business growth.

"The Language of CyberSecurity" is just one of the many avenues through which Jeffrey Rogers shares his wealth of knowledge and experience. Get ready to embark on a journey of discovery and transformation.

Special Thanks

I would like to give a special thanks to all the people I have worked with who helped me on my professional journey. This book would not be possible without your support and the lessons we have learned together. To all the leaders and mentors that I have had the privilege to learn under, thank you for your guidance. I hope this book shows that the lessons have paid off.

A special thanks to my editor, Hollie Kingsland. You are extremely talented and have been very patient throughout this process. Thank you for your expertise.

To my family, thank you for either supporting me or challenging me; both were needed.

I would not be the person I am today without my children, Tre, Jada, Kadiesha, Reagan, and Rylan. I learn from each of you daily; your enthusiasm and curiosity inspire me. You can be whoever you want and do whatever you want at any age. Dream big and follow those dreams.

Lastly, and most importantly, I want to thank my wife, Candace Rogers, for your never-ending support on all of the projects that I take on. You are my soul mate, my cheerleader, my travel agent, and my best friend.

www.ingramcontent.com/pod-product-compliance
Lightning Source LLC
Chambersburg PA
CBHW072134290526
45794CB00004B/1313